To purchase this book or upcoming books by Lisa Dunning, MA, MFT or if you would like Lisa Dunning to speak at your organization visit her website at www.LisaDunningMFT.com

Good Parents
Bad Parenting

How To Parent Together

When Your Parenting Styles

Are Worlds Apart

Lisa Dunning, MA, MFT

ISBN# 1 4116 0420 2

Visit Lisa Dunning at www.LisaDunningMFT.com

Good Parents
Bad Parenting

How To Parent Together

When Your Parenting Styles

Are Worlds Apart

Learn the art of patience.
Apply discipline to your thoughts when they become anxious
over the outcome of a goal.
Impatience breeds anxiety, fear, discouragement and failure.
Patience creates confidence, decisiveness, and a rational
outlook, which eventually leads to success.

Brian Adams

Table of Contents

Foreword

I would first like to thank my parents. You gave me the confidence and strength I needed to be the best parent I could be. You showed me how important it was to be there for my children no matter what. You gave me the strength and encouragement I needed to reach my goals.

I would also like to thank my children for always loving me and forgiving me when I made mistakes. No matter how difficult my day, you could always make me laugh. You showed me the importance of being the best mom I could be.

And to my husband, without your support and encouragement this book would not exist. Thank you for always asking me, "Did you write your book today?" Even though it bothered me at the time, if it wasn't for you, I would not have had the determination to finish our book. Thank you also for being the best dad you could be!

And to my clients, thank you for providing me with years of experiences and the insight necessary to help others. I have the best clients!

And finally to my siblings: See, I told you I could write a book!

Dedicated to my Dad who always believed in me.

1 - Background Of Authors

The worth of a book is to be measured by what you can carry away from it.

James Bryce

Why I Wrote This Book

In my private therapeutic practice I noticed a reoccurring theme from the vast majority of my clients. Session after session, I found myself repeating the same counseling advice with different clients. I thought someone must have written a book about this topic, but when I searched for a book that would adequately address this issue, I surprisingly found nothing. The issue was how to agree when raising their children or as the subtitle expresses more creatively, "How to Parent Together When Your Parenting Styles Are Worlds Apart?" It appears to be a simple concern yet the answer is so complex. The issue is complex because people are so complex. There are the obvious differences between men and women with women generally more open to communicating their feelings than men. Assuming the child is raised by the typical nuclear family with mom and dad living in the same household, mom has a different family history than dad and will obviously have different ideas about how to raise the children than dad. Assuming grandma and grandpa are alive on both sides of the family, their involvement, or lack of involvement, is critical to the development of the children and keep in mind they are from a different generation with completely different opinions and perceptions on how you should be parenting your children. Now let us assume mom and a step dad with his two kids are raising the children and dad lives over an hour away with a girlfriend who is raising a young child. You can see how the complexity can grow. My clients were good parents, wanting to raise happy and responsible children. They merely lacked the communication skills to adequately work through their differences to speak as one voice to their children. Essentially, these were "Good Parents" with "Bad Parenting" skills.

Lisa Asks Brad For Help

When Lisa and I had our first child, a boy, we both were excited and ready to have a child. Although a little scary at first, we eventually settled into the "new parents" roles and learned to bathe, feed, burp and dress the baby.

Conversations involving specific situations such as, "What would you do if our child wanted to get a tattoo?" Or "What will you say if our child wants to sleep at a friends house, but we do not approve of that friend?" became the quickest way to start an argument. In your mind these questions may seem easily answered, but when you ask your partner questions, and you will, prepare for an argument. Assuming you can agree on a given course of action, consider if that course of action would be different if your child is five, twelve, sixteen, or twenty years old? Do you react the same if you are raising a boy or a girl? When Lisa shared with me her desire to write a book to help parents work together when raising their children, I was more than intrigued. I had no idea this issue was such a pervasive problem for parents in her practice. She told me about her ideas for the book and I started adding my input and before long we realized this book would be more beneficial to parents if we wrote the book together. Together we offer both a male and a female perspective. We also offer drastically different familial backgrounds. So throughout this book I offered my perspective when and where I felt it was important. Although generally written as one voice, I want the men, and women, reading this book to understand that many discussions and occasional heated arguments occurred before the final version reached the book you are reading today. If you are a man know that you are represented throughout and this is not purely a woman's perspective about what you should be doing for your wife and kids.

About Brad

I believe it is important to give an understanding of the type of Dad, and person, I am before giving you my perspective on parenting. If you read my short biography and use something to discount my opinions, you are not using this information for its intended purpose. Its purpose is to give you an understanding of who I am along with some of my history, so I can show you that I am a real person with varied interests.

For the purposes of this book I wish I could say I am the typical male, if there is such a thing, but I am not. For the purposes of being a dad, I am proud of the fact that I am not a typical male. I feel I am generally an enlightened man who enjoys learning about things that drive my wife nuts. I watch documentaries, the History and Discovery channels, follow politics and the ongoing middle east problems, watch The O'Reilly Factor, Hannity & Colmes, Star Trek, cartoons with my kids and occasionally I will watch a cartoon on my own. When I watch the high brow shows listed above, my wife says that she married her grandfather. When I watch an occasional cartoon, without the kids, my wife will say she married a child. I enjoy watching professional basketball and tennis. I watch an occasional football game during the regular season and, of course, the Superbowl and I do not watch baseball with the exception of the World Series. I am a good tennis player and play as often as I can, which has dwindled down from three to five times a week before my kids to once a week as my responsibilities increased. I enjoy listening to Blues on guitar and Classic Rock and my favorite band is Pink Floyd. I do not drink beer, but I enjoy a mixed drink on occasion. I am a good husband, but I could be better, and I am a great dad; I have no doubt about that. I am proud of my commitment and abilities as a dad. For this reason I feel my input is important and if my contribution can help just one child have a better childhood, then I am happy to share my history, experiences and moral clarity as a parent to others who may be struggling with their commitment to their children and what being a parent is all about.

How My Wife And I Met

My wife and I met the same way most couple's meet. A collection of strange occurrences led to our chance encounter that led to a couple years of dating, a one year engagement and three years of marriage before our first child. During this entire process I never once considered what life would be like when we had children. Lisa pursued her marriage and family therapist license while I attended college. I worked at a dead end job that basically represented a means to an end: that end usually fell on a Friday when I received a paycheck. One day just lead into another in a series of choices that seemed like the right choices at the time and, on the whole, most of them were good choices and along the way I became a dad.

After the euphoria of these wonderful events wore off, I realized that my wife and I bring some drastically different backgrounds to what needs to be a combined effort in parenting. Then imagine being married to a marriage and family therapist, specializing in parent / child relationship issues. If that does not intimidate most men into a completely submissive role in the parenting process, I don't know what else would. Fortunately my wife has been wonderful about allowing me to throw my two cents into the parenting process while not throwing her education and experience around, except when appropriate.

How My Husband And I Met

When dating, I know the furthest thing from my mind was how my date would rate as a father. My concern was if he showered me with flowers, balloons and attention. As my husband and I became serious about spending the rest of our lives together, I still did not think about being parents. I thought about what kind of provider he would be so I wouldn't have to work all of my life; not so I could stay home with the kids, but so I could go shopping and eat at nice restaurants. Sure we talked about kids. We talked about how many and what their names would be, but we never discussed our parenting beliefs or what type of parents we wanted to be.

Then the wedding arrived. That is when we thought about the possibility of becoming parents. We discussed his family and how he did not wish to repeat the dysfunctional environment. We also discussed my family and how we wanted to repeat the warmth and closeness I felt as a child. We were two people that shared our love for each other yet lived worlds apart when we shared our childhood memories.

Two Parents With Parenting Backgrounds That Are Worlds Apart

As parents we take what we know and lived to guide us when parenting our children. "The first step is to become acquainted with the ghosts in your nursery, the friendly and the not so friendly, and to learn which memories, emotions, and beliefs these ghosts entered through." (Wesselmann 12) Brad and I experienced drastically different backgrounds. How do we combine our worlds so we can agree on our most important issue of raising our children?

This concern has been raised with many of my couples in counseling. As a parent and therapist, I would look for various parenting books that address this concern yet I found most books to be one sided: either written by a man or woman, but not both. I thought how could you get both perspectives if you don't have both sides. And so arrived the birth of "Good Parents Bad Parenting".

You will read both sides: A woman's perspective as well as a man's perspective. You will gain insight from my generally healthy childhood background contrasted with my husband's mostly unhealthy childhood background. A Marriage, Family and Child Therapist, Specializing in Parent/Child Relationship issues educated in theoretical models with years of experience contrasted with my husband's parenting perspective always moving this book toward real world, practical advice.

Why My Husband's Input Is Important

I felt it was important to have a male perspective throughout this book. Men and women are different. To ignore that simple fact and too assume I could adequately represent the male perspective on parenting would be arrogant and unfair to every father. Every man should feel comfortable in the knowledge that my husband and I discussed every topic in this book to be sure the male perspective was adequately represented.

I also felt it was important to provide a perspective from someone who is not in the mental health field. Too often, professionals in the mental health industry can become overly theoretical. My husband continuously reminded me about the importance of striking a balance between my education and the real world, understanding that the vast majority of people reading this book want real life, practical advice.

You may be curious what qualifies my husband to give his perspective throughout this book? My husband's troubled childhood prompted him to read therapy books before we met. His understanding of people and why they do what they do has amazed me. I often tell him he should become a psychotherapist. He jokingly tells me that he would become a therapist if he had a burning desire to work long hours to make very little money.

He also has a degree in Marketing, which involves a tremendous understanding of what it takes to make a potential consumer a customer. Essentially he is always entering the mind of his target market to create an atmosphere that will cause his target audience to take a positive action toward purchasing what he is marketing. If that does not involve a sophisticated level of psychoanalysis, I don't know what else does. Brad conceptualized the title, subtitle and cover design for this book, understanding that without a compelling title, subtitle and cover design, you would not consider buying the book to learn about the quality of its content. But he also understood the importance of quality content that would increase sales when you refer this book to others.

Notes:_____

_____

_____

_____

_____

_____

_____

_____

2 - Establishing The Rules

I hear and I forget.
I see and I remember.
I do and I understand.

Confucius

Allow Yourself To Make Mistakes

"Suggestions found in books, articles, and by the media may cause parents to experience some guilt, doubt, frustration, or anxiety that their disciplinary approach is not right for their child." (Campbell 205) The purpose of this book is not to point out your inadequacies or tell you to follow this book to become the perfect parent(s). After years of education and experience as a therapist and parent I never stop learning how to be a better parent. Reaching a state of perfection would mean I wouldn't need to learn. I learn a new perspective about parenting from my clients, my husband, friends, a good parenting book or from my own family every day.

We Learn From Our Mistakes

Think about the first time you road a bike. I'm sure you didn't just jump on the bike and start riding. You probably fell more than a few times. You felt frustration, anger, hostility, blame, etc. But through falling you also learned determination and eventually the joy of accomplishment when you finally road your bike without falling.

You and anyone who shares the responsibility of raising your child will make mistakes. Hopefully, through your mistakes, you and your partner will learn a great deal about yourself, each other and your child. Learn from your mistakes and try not to repeat them. If you allow a pattern of making the same mistake over and over, then you are not learning.

Allow Your Children To Make Mistakes

You and your partner are allowed to make mistakes but as an adult you must make immediate changes to not repeat the same mistake twice. Since you are allowed to make mistakes then your child should be allowed to make mistakes and in greater quantities. Allow your child to see your imperfections, apologize to your child for them and learn from them. By acknowledging your imperfections and mistakes, your child will acknowledge their imperfections and mistakes. Together you, your partner and your child will make mistakes, acknowledge them and learn how not to repeat them in the future.

Do Not Punish Yourself

You will undoubtedly learn new skills. You will look back at situations where you could have used these skills to make better choices with your child. Don't punish yourself by saying, "Oh, I didn't do it that way." or "Look at all the bad things I have done. I ruined my kid for life!" Depending when you acquired this book, keep in mind it may not have existed when you were making every attempt to raise your child the best you knew how. Assuming it existed and assuming you knew of its existence but chose not to read it, well you made a mistake. You are allowed to make mistakes, . . . remember. Get over it, forgive yourself and learn how you can be a better parent so you don't repeat the mistakes you may have made in the past.

You May Not Agree With Me

This book is a work in progress, as is parenting. My husband and I argue about how to parent from time to time. When two people with different backgrounds are raising a child with a unique personality, disagreement about how to parent appropriately is normal. Taking that perspective a step further, it is also appropriate for you to question my parenting recommendations and methods. My husband and I may make recommendations or use methods that might not be appropriate for you, your unique partner and your unique child. Use the skills and methods that are appropriate for you and your family. Do not use the skills or methods you feel are inappropriate for your family.

Agree To Disagree

We often experience power struggles with our partner when we disagree with their views. Even if they make a good point it is often difficult to let them know they are correct because we are admitting our point was wrong. It is unpleasant enough to be wrong but to let our partner know they were correct is horrible! Do not expect to always agree with your partner. It is reasonable to assume you and your partner will have differing opinions. Life would be boring if you and your partner never had any disagreements. Disagreements are healthy and encouraged. Through the games and exercises in "Good Parents Bad Parenting" you, your partner and your child will learn how to communicate appropriately. You will learn new perspectives about parenting from each other. You will learn the rules of engagement when you and your partner disagree to lessen the potential for a shouting match.

Since there is no time like the present, let's start with a few steps for resolving a conflict. They are:

1. Listen To Your Partner's Point Of View

And I mean really listen whether you agree with your partner or not. Listening to your partner when you agree is easy. Listening when you do not agree is the most difficult time to listen, especially during a heated debate. The goal is to take in what your partner is saying. If you do not understand what your partner is saying, repeat back what you thought your partner said.

2. Express Your Point Of View Appropriately

After listening to your partner it is time for you to express your points. When expressing your points remember to argue the issue. Do not attack your partner. You want your partner to hear your views just like you heard your partner. In order for your partner to hear you, your tone needs to remain calm. If you and your partner are unable to remain calm the goal to learn each other's views will be lost to the detriment of your child.

. Be Mature Enough To Change Your Mind

Remember the importance of the discussion. You and your partner are discussing what is in your child's best interest. You owe it to your child to hear your partner's opinions to make the best possible parenting decision for your child. You and your partner are not competing: you are working as a team.

4. Learn To Compromise

When reading this book, you will undoubtedly discuss these topics with each other and have differing opinions. One of you may agree with me while the other does not. Both of you may agree with each other and disagree with me. Remember that your goal is to make parenting decisions that are in the best interest of your child. Use the best options for your child and compromise on the points that may primarily be in the best interest of you or your partner.

5. Make A Video

This is a great exercise. The only true way for you and your partner to gain an accurate understanding of how you relate to each other and the family is through videotape. Set up a camera in your house where you frequent the most. Eventually you and your family will forget about the camera. After a few days of recording, you and your partner can view the tape. I will warn you now: the camera does not lie. This is the time to work on changing the aspects you do not like.

After discussing your disagreements, if you are unable to arrive at any definitive conclusion, then you may have to ultimately agree to disagree and move on.

Parenting Is Not An Exact Science

In Mathematics, 1 opinion + 1 opinion = 2 opinions and the opinions do not have any consequences beyond their numerical count. But in parenting, 1 opinion + 1 opinion = a lengthy discussion followed by a consequence that will shape the self esteem of your child. Parenting involves opinions, perspectives, feelings and coping skills that sometimes leave you feeling powerless and confused. You will have good days and not so good days while parenting your child. On the good days, you will feel confident in your abilities. On the not so good days, your child will present situations that will confound you and your partner. By having this book in your reach, know you are not alone. My husband and I are here with you, encouraging and cheering you on.

Just Say "No" to "I Told You So"

Some parents have a fear that if one parent wishes to use a harsher consequence than the other and the lesser consequence is administered, resulting in their child repeating the same misbehavior, the parent who sought to use the harsher consequence feels compelled to say, "I told you so!"

The parent who advocated for the less harsh consequence will feel apprehensive about expressing their opinion on consequences in the future. Both parents have to agree not to hold the other's opinions against them when they are wrong. This is not a game of who is the better parent. This is a daily exercise in parenting where the winner or loser is your child.

Your Relationship Ahead Of Your Child

Please do not interpret this section as my advocating the importance of your relationship to the detriment of your child. When taken to extremes it is just as unhealthy to put your child ahead of your relationship with your partner, as it is to put your relationship with your partner ahead of your child. You should always take time to cultivate your relationship with your partner. "For married fathers, if you want to connect with your kids, the first place to start is by making sure you are connected with your wife or partner. " (Levine and Pittinsky 162) Putting your relationship first sounds selfish and un parent like. So, why is a therapist telling you to put your relationship needs ahead of your child's needs?

- Which Came First, The Relationship Or Your Child?

  In the vast majority of families the relationship came first. Without the relationship, you would not have your child. Yes I know that you can become pregnant without being in a relationship, but for a truly healthy family life, the relationship needs to be strong. If there are problems within the relationship, your child will suffer.

- Always Putting Your Child 1st Can Harm Your Child

  If you find yourself uncomfortable with this concept and do not believe what I am telling you to be true, ask children of divorce, "If you could have one wish, what would it be?" The majority of them will say for their parents to get back together. Most children of divorce often blame themselves and feel that if only they were better children their parents would still be together. Because of this feeling, children of divorce often suffer tremendous guilt, depression, anger and low self image.

  When the relationship suffers, the tendency for parents to verbally attack each other will rise. This has a negative effect on the children. Children in a hostile environment will become hostile themselves. You may notice an increase in aggressive behavior with siblings and peers. You and your partner are the first relationship your children will ever know. They will believe other people interact the way you and your partner interact. Therefore, you owe it to your children to put your relationship first and teach them appropriate ways to relate to others. The conclusions they formulate about relationships based on your relationship with your partner will become the blueprint for all their future relationships. A healthy blueprint will produce a healthy relationship. An unhealthy blueprint will produce an unhealthy relationship. If you or your partner verbally attacks around your children, you are teaching your children inappropriate ways to express their feelings.

• Prepare For The Day Your Child Moves Out
    Another important reason you and your partner should put your relationship first is to prepare for the day your children move out. When this time arrives you do not want to be living with a stranger. The "empty nest" syndrome is a difficult transition and you will need the support of your partner. It will be more difficult to get through this transition if your partner is a stranger.

Now that you are aware of the importance of putting your relationship first, here are some ways that you and your partner can continue to strengthen your relationship:

- Make time for the relationship. Go out to dinner, a movie, or just stay home without the children.

- Communicate with each other. Make sure you check in with each other every day. Do not take each other for granted. Ask your partner if they had a good day and really be interested in the events of their day. Fill them in on the eventful moments of your day.

- Do not hold grudges. Talk about your feelings and frustrations with your partner.

- Rekindle the romance. Put notes around the house or in your partner's wallet, briefcase, etc.

- Communicate your relationship goals with your partner.

- Support each other.

Strengthening your relationship is a daily challenge. If it were easy there would be fewer divorces. Working on your relationship with your partner should be as much work as parenting your children and equally rewarding.

Communicating With Your Partner

Communication is the key to a successful marriage and parenting. This concept is so simple and yet most divorces occur due to a breakdown in communication. We will often communicate our thoughts in a way others cannot understand. How many times do you hear women say, "Why should I tell my husband how I feel? He should already know how I feel?" I could have avoided numerous misunderstandings and hurt feelings in my relationship with my husband if I did not assume he knew what I was thinking. This form of miscommunication primarily stems from the patterns that develop between partners over time and the longer the relationship; the more established the patterns and therefore the greater the opportunity for an assumed pattern of behavior to be the cause of an argument. "Of course he should know what I am thinking. I only sent out every non verbal cue to express my desire for him to respond the way I know he should. How could he have missed them? They were as clear as a bell to me!" The plain truth about communication is NOBODY can read minds. Only through appropriate communication and listening skills can you really understand what is going on inside another person's mind. As I tell my children everyday, "Use your words." Be clear about what you really want and state it in an appropriate manner. You will avoid a lot of misunderstandings, arguments and hurt feelings. As the old saying goes, "Don't assume, because assuming will only make an "ass" out of "u" and "me".

Appropriate Communication Between You And Your Partner

Now that you understand the importance of communicating, the next step is to learn how we communicate. Learning appropriate communication is so important because your children will learn from you and your spouse's behavior. If you do not like how your children speak to you, or if you do not like that your children are not speaking to you at all, look at how you and your spouse relate to one another. Do you talk at each other? Do you blame each other? Do you yell or use the "silent treatment"? Your children emulate all of these actions. If you want your children to discuss what is happening in their lives, then you must learn to be open with your feelings. The first place to learn effective communication skills is with your spouse. If your child observes how approachable, open minded and attentive you are to your spouse, they will feel more comfortable coming to you with their issues. If they feel you are explosive, judgmental, closed minded and aloof they will generally not approach you with their issues.

Do Not Blame!

Communicate with your partner without assigning blame. If your spouse feels verbally attacked, they will mentally and emotionally shut down from what you are trying to convey.

For your spouse to really hear what you are saying, an effective communication skill is called "I messages." This method of communicating explains your feelings to your spouse without feeling threatened or blamed. Here is an example of an "I message":

When you (*explain a situation that just happened*), I feel (*attach a feeling word i.e. sad, angry, agitated, etc.*) because (*state why you feel this feeling*). Instead what I would like you to do is (*state what you would like from your partner*).

This form of communication is good to use with your spouse, children, boss, co workers, etc. It is an effective form of communication because it enables the recipients to clearly hear what you are feeling and it allows them to clearly understand what you would like from them. If you only use portions of the "I message" technique, you are not clearly communicating to your partner. Be sure to clearly convey the entire "I message" technique to your partner. Do not be vague! If you are unable to clearly convey an entire "I message" technique to your partner, take the time to think about your "I message" so it is clear in your mind what you want to say to your partner. Taking the time to think about exactly what you want to say in your "I message" will facilitate a more productive discussion of what you do not like and what you expect from your partner in the future.

Debate The Issue, Not Your Spouse

The way you communicate can make or break your relationships. Communication is the tool that is needed in order to convey your thoughts and ideas. If you are argumentative, aggressive, hostile, irrational, judgmental and abusive, your partner will not hear your thoughts and ideas and will only feel attacked. When you are communicating a point remember to debate the issue and not your spouse.

Be Aware Of Your Insecurities

Every parent has a different definition of appropriate parenting. An insecure parent can feel threatened if anyone challenges his or her interpretation of appropriate parenting. When their views are challenged, insecurities can rise to the surface causing the parent to become defensive and closed minded. Follow the recommendations in "Good Parents Bad Parenting" to minimize the potential for insecurities in yourself as well as others.

Good Parents Are A Team

You are not enemies. This is not a competition. You are a team! Teams win when working together. Be receptive to each other. Appreciate what you and your partner have to offer. Utilize each other's strengths. Compensate for each other's weaknesses. You and your partner have the same goal: to provide your child with the tools necessary to thrive in their relationships, their careers and the world.

I'm Not Trying To Be Politically Correct, Just Marketable

Now I use the word, "partner" throughout this book not because I am trying to be politically correct. I use the phrase "partner" because just as easily as a married couple raising their own biological child could read this book, a single mom living with a recently divorced dad could be raising her child in his house everyday and parenting his children every other weekend. I wanted to use terminology that would encompass as many different parenting situations as could possibly exist and the word "partner" seems the most appropriate. I also use "spouse" where appropriate as well.

Brad Explains The Difference Between Being a "Dad" vs. Being a "Father"

Throughout this book I make reference to the terms, "Father" and "Dad". I use the quotation marks to clearly convey that I am using these terms with my specific definition in mind. Allow me to explain the difference so you can understand why I use these terms the way I do.

It is easy to spot a "Father": A "Father" pretends to spend time with their children. They come into a room during special occasions and pick up each child, posing for pictures and then never interact with the kids again until the next special occasion. This keeps the illusion of a "Dad" alive and well in photo albums. "Dad"'s, on the other hand, come into a room on a daily basis and pick up their kids when there is not a camera around. "Dad"'s read books, "Dad"'s play games, "Dad"'s sing inanely simple kids songs and learn to like them a little, "Dad"'s dance with every one of their children just "one more time" until his arms are exhausted. "Dad"'s struggle to answer the steady stream of questions about the world and how it works in age appropriate answers. Fathers never have to worry about missing an important game on television because someone is watching the kids. "Father"'s work long hours because they want to get ahead in their careers or want to make some extra money or because they do not like going home to their family. "Dad"'s work long hours because they need to make more money to support their family and wish they did not need to work those long hours so they could spend more time at home with their kids. At some point you make your choice to be a "Dad" or a "Father". I made my choice the day my son was born and I never looked back. I have a difficult time understanding "Father"'s who do not want to spend time with their children and I suppose you might think that I am overly critical of "Father"s who are not "Dad"s. It is easy for me to be a "Dad" and I do judge "Father"s harshly, but I also appreciate and openly commend "Dad"s as well.

The Goal Of "Good Parents Bad Parenting"

The first goal of "Good Parents Bad Parenting" is to provide you with the insight to acknowledge your history, keep the aspects of your history you like and drop the baggage you and your partner do not wish to pass on to your children.

The second goal of "Good Parents Bad Parenting" is to improve communication with your partner so you can agree on how to raise a responsible, cooperative and successful child.

And the third goal of "Good Parents Bad Parenting" is to provide practical advice on a wide range of topics to improve your ability to parent with your partner more effectively. Every chapter in "Good Parents Bad Parenting" has been explored in great detail in referenced material at the back of the book. Brad and I encourage you to read the referenced material, as the materials will provide additional insight and context behind the parenting advice provided in "Good Parents Bad Parenting".

Notes:_____

_____

_____

_____

_____

_____

_____

_____

_____

3 - Advice For New Parents

A baby is God's opinion that the world should go on.

Carl Sandberg

Discipline Is Easier If You Start From Day One

Believe it or not, you begin disciplining your child from day one. A newborn's form of communication is through crying. Crying is your baby's way of telling you they are hungry, need a new diaper, do not feel well or would like your attention. By responding to your baby's cries you are reinforcing the baby's behavior. If the baby's needs are not met the baby will continue to cry.

You have undoubtedly heard many experts on the topic of sleeping. Some experts advocate allowing your baby to cry until they sleep; others advocate your baby sleeping in your bed; and some will say pick them up as soon as they cry. The ultimate choice is yours. Whatever you choose there will be consequences. You and your partner are setting limits with your baby. You are structuring how much freedom your child will be given within limits.

Babies Cry Because They Cannot Speak

A baby can only communicate through crying. If you do not respond to your baby, you are teaching your baby that what they want is not important. "Some parents have been told that if you pick up a baby and he or she stops crying, you will be encouraging the infant to cry in the future. In my opinion, that is nonsense! In fact, just the opposite occurs; the child cries less and learns to communicate with cooing sounds." (Owens 2) I'm not saying to pick up your baby as soon as your baby cries. I'm not saying to drop everything to attend to their needs. What I am saying is that it is important that your baby's needs are met. If you do not respond to your baby's cries in a timely manner, your baby will learn that crying will not result in their needs being met and an opportunity to establish trust between you and your baby will be lost. Your baby will eventually stop crying because they have learned their needs will not be met when they cry, so why bother crying. Babies thrive on interaction and contact. If you want your child to learn trust, then you need to be there for your child. "Raising children is about establishing positive relationships between caregivers and their offspring, and the optimal time to begin cultivating a solid relationship is in infancy." (Owens 19) Pick up your baby when they cry, hold them, love them and run down the list of possible reasons for their crying. Even if you are unable stop your baby from crying, they know you are comforting them and this will enable your baby to trust and love you.

The only time where you need to stay away from your baby when they cry is when their crying has reached a point where you feel compelled to hurt your baby. When you feel overwhelmed, leave your baby in a safe place and get away from your baby to allow yourself time to calm down. Do not return until you are able to attend to your baby without fear of losing control.

You Cannot Spoil A Baby

It is important to know that you cannot spoil a baby. Many people think that by holding your baby or fulfilling your baby's needs, you will spoil them. THIS IS ABSOLUTELY NOT TRUE! "In order for children to develop positive self esteem in the social domain, infants must develop strong emotional bonds with their principal caregiver and learn to develop a sense of trust in others." (Owens 28) Your baby is only a baby for a short period of time, so enjoy holding them and kissing them while you can. When your child is older, you may regret missing the opportunity to love, cuddle and hold your baby. And after all, how can too much love be a bad thing?

Discipline Is Difficult If You Start After Year One

As your baby begins to grow and explore the world, you set new limits in order to protect your child from harm. "Because parents socialize their children through the establishment of rules and communication patterns in the family, the degree and quality of parental control and involvement have a major impact on adolescent development. " (Sartor and Youniss) The mistake many parents make is thinking that discipline and consequences come much later for the child. If your child is aware of their limits from day one, your child will understand and learn what is expected from them as they grow.

This Dad's Advice To Dads About "Boring" Babies

I like to teach my children, instill some wisdom, and show them how the world works. Some men have a hard time relating to infants because they typically do not do anything but eat, sleep and cry. How can you teach an infant? I used to take my son for long walks in a snuggly and let him touch all of the flowers, plants and trees. I would tell him the names of things he saw, felt or held. I read books and played all kinds of music for him. Doing some, any or all of these things with your child feels good and can only be good for your child. If you do all of these things with your child and are still having a difficult time, I can offer only this. I understand how difficult that time can be for some men. What I say to those future Dads is "Be ready." Stay as involved with that "boring" infant as much as possible so you are ready to take a more proactive role when that baby becomes less "boring".

Enjoy Being A Parent

When I had my first child, I joined many classes to meet and spend a great deal of time around other first time parents. Many moms would complain about the sleepless nights, constant crying and the pure exhaustion of being a parent. These moms would also complain that they have no time for themselves. When asked about their spouse, the moms would often say that their husbands could not change a diaper, give their child a bath, feed, dress or put their child to bed.

Curious about these "inept" fathers I observed these same mothers controlling how these "inept" fathers would care for their child. After a few months of continuous observation, I observed these same mothers caring for their children while complaining about their husband's passive role. It was clear these fathers had been stripped of their ability to parent and lacked the confidence to care for their child. They relinquished their active parenting role so as not to be ridiculed by their wives.

Allow Your Husband To Parent

I love being a parent but I also love to have some time to myself. Sometimes as mothers we forget that we matter too. In order to enjoy some alone time, you need to let a few things go. So the baby's diaper leaked. I never heard of a baby dying from being wet. So the baby's outfit does not match. The baby usually will spit up on it anyway. So your husband puts the baby to sleep at a different time or washes the baby a different way than you. Just be thankful that you have a spouse who is involved in your child's life. Learn to let go of the control and enjoy the interaction your child is having with their dad. Remember that you are both equally important to your child's well being. When your husband is spending one on one time with your child, it is your time to take care of yourself.

Brad Says, "Get In The Game!"

Generally men feel more disconnected from the parenting process and in large part because women tend to view their job as the parent to raise the child, whether innately, from social pressures, or whatever you have heard experts say are the reasons. Fortunately my wife and I do raise our kids together and we have a pretty good system of debating what is best for our children. I tell her what I think; she says, "No." I tell her my reasons why I think my ideas are good and she gives the appearance of listening to me and then says, "No." again. I do some research on the topic and present her with more ideas about my thoughts and she says, "Let me think about it." A couple weeks later she says, "No." I am kidding of course, but if I can convey two very important points to my fellow dads out there it would be the following. Always remember that women need to let their husbands be dads. Dads have to remember that this is your child too and if you love your child, then you will argue with your wife, tooth and nail, to be heard. If you fight to be heard but you feel you are talking to a brick wall, then I would recommend you give her this book and highlight the important parts that may help your cause and see if that helps. If that still does not change her attitude, then seeking professional help would be appropriate and necessary in the best interest of you, your marriage and your child. The alternative is to do nothing, allow her to raise the children while you feel increasing resentment toward her, doing damage to your marriage and the relationship you have with your children.

You Are Parents For Life, Not 18 Years

It takes two to make a baby and therefore, takes two to raise your baby. When you and your spouse decide to have a baby, it is a lifetime commitment. You will be parents for the rest of your life. The responsibility does not end when your child turns eighteen; it just changes. "Parents do not 'own' their children but are responsible for promoting their well being." (Justice and Justice 1 5) The decision to have children should not be taken lightly. Both partners need to agree on having a child because having a child will forever change your life, hopefully for the better!

Notes:_____

_____

_____

_____

_____

_____

_____

_____

4 - Stay At Home Parenting vs. Financial Concerns

Money cannot buy peace of mind.
It cannot heal ruptured relationships,
or build meaning into a life that has none.

Richard M. DeVos

Congratulations on becoming a parent! Now you look at your bundle of joy and wonder what life was like before your baby. You probably check to see if the baby is breathing at night. When you hold your baby, it probably is difficult to imagine being separated, but you are near the end of your maternity leave and you must decide between staying home or returning to the work force.

I remember when my oldest child was an infant sleeping in his crib. I would stare at him and feel overwhelmed and overjoyed at his innocence and how dependent he was on me, and my husband, to fulfill his every need. I knew no one would love my child or take care of him the way my husband and I could. It was important for me to stay home to take care of our child. My husband and I agreed that we would do everything we could to raise our children. Although we have had to endure some tough financial times, we never regret our decision to keep our children out of the care of others. Only occasional babysitters, aunts, uncles and grandparents have cared for our children for short periods of time.

If you and your partner agree as my husband and I agreed, the decision to stay home or return to work is easy. But what happens when you want to stay home and you and your partner already had an agreement that you would return to work?

Your partner deserves to hear your point of view as well as your change in plans. Before making any decisions, discuss why it is important for you to stay home with your partner. Explain your feelings and your reasons for not returning to work. A purely emotional argument will certainly lead directly to a shouting match and a breakdown in communication. Your feelings are important and should be a major part of your argument, but to argue effectively to your husband on this issue, you need to understand how men think and argue. Men remove their emotions from the decision making process. A persuasive argument filled with good points is what a man wants to hear. Anticipate his concerns and prepare your responses to his questions. Typically the main concern is how the family will survive without two incomes. It is very difficult in today's economy to survive on one income. Most families cannot afford to live on one income, but if you wish to stay home to raise your child, you must get creative. With some creativity it can be done. You might need to move into a smaller home or less expensive area. Your partner might have to find a more lucrative job, if possible, or you might have to rely on your family for some financial support. Research the benefits of staying home to care for your child and outline a plan that will address his potential concerns. Regardless of what it takes, if you want to be a stay at home parent, you and your spouse need to discuss ways you can obtain this goal. A persuasive argument with a focus on logical reasons for your not returning to work will increase the likelihood to garner your husband's support rather than purely an emotional argument. Write out estimates of day care, gas, work clothes, lunches, etc. Then compare your estimate with your income. If the disparity is small you can make a strong argument for staying home. If that still does not work, look into jobs that will allow you to work from home. Contact the work at home opportunities before speaking with your husband. If you can find work that allows you to stay home before your maternity leave is exhausted, your husband will be more inclined to agree with your decision if money is already flowing into the house before you announce your plan to stay home. Be careful of gimmicks. Remember if it sounds too good to be true it probably is!

Your Partner Cannot Read Minds

More arguments occur when a wife says, "I shouldn't have to tell him how I'm feeling. He should already know." Ladies, I am telling you with emphasis, "OUR HUSBANDS CAN NOT READ OUR MINDS!" It is important for you and your spouse to sit down together and discuss all of your wants and needs about being a stay at home mom. Remember to be calm even if the conversation is not going your way. If you feel anxious and stressed, take a ten minute break and return to your conversation after you have composed yourself. Always remember that you are a team. You are not enemies. You both want the best for your family. You just have different visions of how to accomplish this goal. If all else fails and you both are dissatisfied, work on a compromise. Maybe you will work part time or full time for only a few months so you can save. When a decision is reached that satisfies your wants and his concerns, outline your plan with specific dates and goals. Revisit these expected dates and goals periodically to avoid unexpected surprises or assumptions. Obviously if a key date or financial goal becomes unattainable or is attained earlier than expected, it would make sense to discuss how to modify your financial plan. Listen to each other and be flexible but firm in the pursuit of your ultimate financial and maternal goals.

Looking Into Daycare

If a stranger approaches you and your partner on the street, asking to hold your child, I hope you would say, "GET LOST!" Then why would you trust a daycare facility without researching and scrutinizing every potential daycare facility and its personnel before handing your child over to a complete stranger? You and your partner agree to put your child in daycare. It is the best alternative for your family situation. I cannot emphasize enough that you and your partner need to interview and research potential daycare facilities that you are intending to care for your most precious gift, your child.

Many people put their child in a day care facility for all the wrong reasons. For the time you and your partner are away, this daycare facility and its staff are parenting your child. Can you trust this facility with the life of your child? Convenient hours, cost, proximity to your home or work, lunch and diaper services or any other logistical consideration should be far down the list of priorities for choosing a daycare facility. Look into references of the provider. Ask other parents how their children like the facility. Visit the facility often and without notice to learn how your child is being treated on an average day when they do not expect a visit. If you feel uncomfortable or notice any signs that things are not right, trust your instincts and pull your child out of the facility. It is better to be safe than sorry. If the facility does not like the surprise visits, pull your child out of the facility immediately and look for a new facility. This is your child's life! You have every right to visit your child's school unannounced. You have every right to research the facility and ask intrusive and uncomfortable questions. You are entrusting your child to this facility. For the time you and your partner are not caring for your child, the daycare facility is your child's parent.

When you observe the facility observe how the daycare staff are interacting with the children. "Children receiving care of high quality have superior relationship skills, whereas children receiving care of poor quality have deficient social skills and may behave more aggressively than children without such experiences." (Lamb 46) Are they playing with your child on his, or her, level? Does the childcare staff seem warm and nurturing? How do they handle conflict between two children? Do the children seem happy and involved in creative and developmental activities? Some other considerations are:

- Is the facility safe and clean?

- Are the children ages appropriate for your child?

- What is the child to adult ratio?

- Is the facility licensed?

- Does the facility provide criminal background checks for all employees?

- Have there been any complaints or has the facility been cited for inadequacies?

- What is their method for disciplining a child?

- Obviously look for facilities that do not utilize corporal punishment.

- What are there security procedures for monitoring child pickup?

- Do they have an earthquake or other catastrophic emergency plan?

- Is the staff educated in early childhood development?

Be sure to have all of these considerations and any additional considerations unique to your child or situation addressed completely before choosing a daycare facility. Do not trust these strangers with your child until they have shown they are to be trusted.

Reversing The Roles: Mom Is Working And Dad Is Parenting At Home

More moms are returning to work with dad staying home to raise the children. When mom has the ability to bring home a larger paycheck or dad is better equipped to care for the children; this is a wonderful way to allow the children to be raised by their parents and not by daycare. However this arrangement can cause some marital problems.

The problems arise when mom comes home after a hard day at work and then needs to cook the meals, do the laundry, clean the house, give the kids a bath, etc. If you are feeling overworked and frustrated talk to your spouse. Express your concerns and frustrations appropriately. Also remember to express your wants. You might not get all of your needs met but at least you will feel heard.

Meanwhile, dad is not feeling appreciated for all of his hard work while mom is away. Dad can become tired of play dates with other stay at home moms and may miss the office chitchat with other male co workers. Dad might also feel the pressure of performing tasks that are traditionally performed by a woman. Some men measure their value by their jobs and their income. There is not any monetary compensation for being a stay at home dad and the position does not offer an opportunity to move up, although it does offer some opportunity for growth. Strangely enough, primarily men and some women tend to view a working mom and dad with a child in daycare more favorably than a woman working and a man staying home to raise the children, believing there must be something wrong with him if the wife is the breadwinner. Basically American society tends to view a stay at home dad as a failing father, resulting in an undesirable and unwelcome situation by both the mom and the dad.

Enjoy both of your new roles. Remember why you made the decision to switch roles. It was most likely because it was in the best interest of your family. So when you both are really stressed, remember that you are doing what is best for your family.

A Stay At Home Dad Pep Talk

Being a stay at home dad is great! I earned my marriage and family therapist license a few months before I gave birth to my first child. I stayed home to take care of my child as my husband and I worked very hard to make my private practice a reality. Initially I did not have many clients, which meant I was essentially a stay at home mom while my husband worked a full time job to bring home a paycheck. With a great deal of marketing effort from my husband and networking on my part, my practice grew to a point where we decided my husband would become a stay at home dad. So when I express my views on stay at home dads, please know that I am speaking from experience as a stay at home mom and a wife to a stay at home dad. All stay at home moms can appreciate the hard work involved when raising a child 24 hours a day, days a week. It is one of the hardest jobs you will ever love. So if you are a stay at home dad, say it with confidence. You should never feel ashamed for making your children your highest priority.

Notes:_____

_____

_____

_____

_____

_____

_____

_____

_____

5 - Clean Out The Baggage

You must be the change you wish to see in the world.

Mahatma Gandhi

You and your partner came from two distinct family backgrounds. Both of you were raised differently, which influences your parenting styles today. By learning your family history you are less likely to repeat negative parenting behaviors and more likely to implement positive parenting behaviors.

The first step is to explore your childhood and that of your spouse to understand what type of parents your parents were. I know this seems tedious and overwhelming to go this far back, but you are who you are because of the experiences and challenges in your life and they stem back to your family of origin. You and your partner can do a family history to gain a clearer understanding of what patterns exist in your family.

This is a terrific exercise to gain an understanding of your history and the history of your spouse. It also will allow you and your spouse to do an activity together to try to resolve any existing parenting disagreements. Use your notes section at the end of this chapter to create your family history. You are looking for relationship interactions, history of divorce, abuse, alcohol and drug abuse and history of mental illness. You may discover other patterns that are not mentioned here. When filling in your family history answer the following questions:

- How did your grandparents/parents relate to each other in terms of abuse, arguing or being distant?
- Did they communicate appropriately or did they yell or abuse each other either physically or mentally?
- Is there a history of divorce and remarriage(s)?
- Were your parents/grandparents affectionate toward each other?
- How was affection shown?
- What was your happiest memory?
- What was your saddest memory?
- Was there any financial/job instability?
- What role did education play in the family?

- What role did religion play in the family?

- How did the grandparents/parents relate to the children?

- Were they abusive either physically or emotionally?

- Were the children made to feel a part of, or apart from, the family?

- Did the children fear one grandparent/parent?

- Who disciplined the children and what type of discipline was used?

- Were there any drug, alcohol, tobacco, and food addictions in the family?

- Is there a history of mental illness such as depression, anxiety, phobias, suicide, etc.?

This exercise is a good tool for you and your partner to understand your family history and how that history has played a role in the person, spouse and parent you are today. Finding patterns is important because you and your partner have to find a way to break the inappropriate patterns that have plagued your family for generations. Your family history is like a blueprint of your past and your future if you were to do nothing to change it. Now that you are aware of the patterns, you can actively work to create more appropriate patterns. Your children will inherit these patterns and will pass them on to their children, breaking the dysfunction cycle. "Warm, loving feeling memories of the past can make parents feel as if they are in touch with their own natural parental instincts   although their 'natural instincts' are in actuality a 'ghostly' gift from their loving parents." (Wesselmann 11)

The next step is to discover new patterns that you want to create with your new family. This is where you and your partner decide what is, and is not, acceptable behavior and how you are going to provide a loving, nurturing, supportive, and structured environment for your new family. This step will take years to accomplish and is a goal that you will always be working to obtain. If you, or your partner, lose sight of your goals you can revisit your family history in order to get back on track. Every three months you and your partner can make a new family history to re evaluate who is being impacted by the changes you have implemented. You can reexamine how you and your partner are relating to each other? Has any inappropriate interactions decreased between you and your partner? How are you relating to your children? Who is providing the discipline and what types of discipline are being used? Are you getting the results you expected? Looking for areas where you could improve communication skills and family interactions to reduce tension in your family will be a continuing goal.

Notes:_____

_____

_____

_____

_____

_____

_____

_____

6 - Three Parenting Styles

He who knows others is wise.
He who knows himself is enlightened.

Lao Tzu,

"Because parents socialize their children through the establishment of rules and communication patterns in the family, the degree and quality of parental control and involvement have a major impact on adolescent development." (Sartor and Youniss) Every parent has a different interpretation or perception of parenting. Disagreement occurs when one partner does not agree with the consequence the other spouse implemented. One partner may have been raised in an environment where spanking was administered as the primary form of punishment. The common argument is, "Well I was spanked as a child and I grew up okay." The other parent may not believe in the use of spanking, or may believe spanking should only be used as a last resort in favor of less aggressive forms of discipline. Obviously these are two extremely different interpretations of parenting with each parent expressing a drastically different viewpoint and approach to administering consequences. Your disagreements probably fall somewhere in between these two extremes. To resolve this argument or a similar argument between parents, a better understanding of the different styles of parenting is necessary so both parents can have a common framework from which to begin a dialogue. Only after a complete understanding of these styles can a meaningful dialogue begin and ultimately a resolution.

Controlling Parent

There are three distinct parenting styles. As a child did you hear the phrase, "Because I'm the parent and I said so!" This style of parenting provides the child with no freedom, which in turn, creates an environment of no personal growth. The child is not in an environment where they can learn. They are being told what to do without an understanding of why they need to do what they are told.

Passive Parent

The second style of parenting is the Passive Parent. This type of parenting style allows the child to rule the house. You have probably witnessed children who seem like they make the rules of the house and tell their parents what to do. This style of parenting creates an environment where there is no limit setting and no structure, which creates an environment where the child does not respect himself or authority. Without respect for authority children of passive parents cannot teach their children appropriate behavior.

Reasonable Parent

The third style of parenting is the Reasonable Parent. This style of parenting sets limits with a firm and calm approach. The parent provides choices for the child, which enables the child to learn from the consequences of their choices without fear or threats from the parent. This environment provides freedom within limits. This form of parenting increases self esteem, allows your child to learn from their choices, helping them to become respectful, responsible and courageous individuals. (Popkin 14)

What Type Of Parenting Style Did Your Parents Implement?

Think back to when you were a child. What type of parenting style did your parents implement? Then ask your partner the same question. Here are some questions that might help you find the parenting style your parents used:

Category 1:

1. Did you hear the phrase: "Wait until your father comes home?"

2. Did you fear one or both parents?

4. Did you feel that you could go to your parents and not feel judged, blamed, lectured, etc?

. Did your parents spank you?

4. Were your punishments severe? (Being grounded for a month, no car for 6 weeks, etc.)

5. Did your parents use threats?

6. Did you engage in shouting matches?

   If you answered yes to most of these questions then you grew up in a parent controlling household.

Category 2:

1. Did you break rules without any consequences?

2. Did your parents seem to fear you?

. Did you get into trouble with authority figures?

4. Did you seem to make your own rules?

5. Did you feel the world owed you?

6. Did you appear to run the household?

   If you answered yes to most of these questions then you grew up in a passive household.

Category :

1. Did you feel your consequences fit the "crime"?

2. Did you feel your parents listened to you?

. Did you feel like you had choices?

4. Did you feel that you could go to your parents and not feel judged, blamed, lectured, etc?

5. Did you have freedom within limits?

6. Did you have high self esteem?

If you answered yes to most of these questions then you were raised in a household that used a reasonable style of parenting.

Learning The Parenting Styles That Raised You

This exercise is important for several reasons. The style of parenting under which you were raised is often carried over to the style of parenting you will favor. " . . . you may be a new parent, or even a prospective parent, already aware that you may be missing the so called "natural instincts" for healthy parenting that others talk about. You may find yourself feeling more confused and anxious about your new role as parent than you would like." (Wesselmann 10) If you were raised in a family that implemented a reasonable style of parenting, you will probably raise your children in a reasonable style of parenting. If you were raised in a controlling or passive family household, you have a lot of hard work ahead of you. You will have to fight your instincts to change and continually work with your parenting partner to be sure you are not making decisions that are leading you back into a passive or controlling style of parenting.

Learning The Parenting Styles That Raised Your Partner

Once you explore the style of parenting that raised you, it is now time to explore the parenting style under which your partner was raised. This enables both of you to communicate about how each of you were raised and the parenting style you would like to use with your children.

Taking a family history is a great way for the two of you to gain an understanding of your different family histories and to find ways to come together and make a new history with your children. (See: Cleaning Out The Baggage in Chapter)

Adopt A Parenting Style

After determining the parenting style under which you were raised, the next step is to determine what parenting style you want for your children. On paper, the ideal parent is the Reasonable Parent. This style enables you and your partner to offer choices. Your child will learn from the consequences of their choices. However you might find that the Controlling or Passive parenting style is more appropriate is more suited to your needs. Whichever style you choose, continually ask yourself, "What is the goal of parenting and what do we need to do to obtain this goal?"

The best way to determine a parenting style is to determine what types of personality traits both of you have. How many times do we hear the phrase, "opposites attract"? Well, having opposite parenting styles might not be so attractive. In fact, it can cause many arguments later in the relationship. If you are a controlling person who always takes charge and likes things your way, then that is most likely the parenting style you will implement. If you marry a person who is very passive in their decision making, then chances are your partner will implement a passive parenting style. In this type of relationship, both will need to sit down and explore when the controlling or passive style is appropriate for a unique situation or child. If you combine these two traits appropriately, you will create a reasonable parenting style. The whole goal is to communicate with each other and explore your personalities to determine how they can be combined into one cohesive parenting style.

This Dad's Parenting Style

I believe my style is a conscious choice I made to be the dad I wish I had. Parenting is not an exact science and sometimes I make choices I later wish I had not made, but on the whole I would say I am very confident about my ability to parent. I would definitely say that I am stricter with our children than my wife. I'm quicker to nip undesirable behavior with less warning: sometimes that style works well and sometimes it does not. The advantage of my style is that our children generally respond to my requests faster than my wife. The disadvantage of my style is that I can be a little too quick to discipline when a little coaxing may have been a more appropriate way to elicit the desired behavior. In general I will say this about the times when your overall style is different than your partner. Do not do anything behind your partner's back that contradicts what your partner and you agreed. Talk about your differences a lot, talk about why you believe your approach is best, talk about why you think her approach is not the best. Remember that you both have your child's best interest at heart and it is not a competition to see who can raise the better child or who is the better parent. You are both raising this child and will receive a combined grade for your efforts. Appreciate the fact that your partner may get upset at what you have to say about her parenting style versus yours; it means she cares about the well being of your child. Or she is thinking that you are an idiot and that she was an idiot to marry you. Or she is scared you are calling her an inadequate mother who should not be raising a child. Sadly any one of these could be true and perhaps some other psychological perspectives I had not considered may be true as well, but none of these possibilities should prevent you from voicing your opinion when it involves the well being of your child.

Notes:_____

_____

_____

_____

_____

_____

_____

_____

_____

7 - Agreeing On Discipline

*The ultimate test of a relationship
is to disagree but hold hands.*

Alexander Penney

Single parents have an advantage as they do not have to coordinate their discipline efforts with another person. It is hard enough to discipline your child alone but how do you and your partner discipline together? In order for the household to seem together and in unison, the children always need to feel both parents are in agreement with each other, even if behind closed doors you are not. "Children need and want parental guidance while being treated with love and respect. Disciplinary rules should not be abstract, complex, or unclear. " (Campbell 205) So, how do you agree on appropriate discipline for your child when you can not agree to watch the same television shows, where to eat, the color to paint the living room, etc.

Define The Goal Of Your Consequence

This sounds complicated and overwhelming, but the answer to disciplining together is to first define the goal of your consequence. In other words, what behavior do you wish to extinguish and what outcome do you wish to promote. Hopefully, you and your partner agree that the choice your child made was inappropriate. When you discuss an appropriate consequence with your partner and present your case, make sure you remain calm yet firm. Should you feel your stress level increasing, take a 10 minute break and come back to the conversation when you feel you can continue at a reasonably calm level. The goal is to have your partner listen to you and understand your point of view. Once you present your side it is time for you to listen to your partner. Remember that if you want to be heard, then you need to listen to your partner. If you still cannot agree, then explain to your partner that you understand their points but still feel your child needs to be disciplined, or not disciplined, for their actions. It is acceptable to disagree passionately but it is unacceptable to yell and berate each other. I understand this is easier said than done, but necessary for the well being of your child. It is important for you and your partner to use appropriate communication skills to set a good example for your child. If you want your child to listen and be respectful to you and others, then you and your partner need to find a way to listen and be respectful to each other especially when you disagree. (See: Agree To Disagree in Establishing The Rules in Chapter 2)

Communicating Your Differences With Little Success

"Given parents in a marriage with a good deal of unresolved conflict, it seems understandable that some of their frustration will spill over into their relationships with the children." (Cowan and Cowan 156) If you and your partner have tried communicating in an appropriate manner, but neither side is willing to listen and compromise, I would conclude these differences go a lot deeper than the issue of discipline. Your couple relationship might need some fine tuning. You and your partner might consider seeking a mental health professional to assist you with relationship issues.

Now Comes The Consequence

For your child to learn from their mistakes, the consequence needs to "fit the crime". If the consequence is too severe or does not relate to the inappropriate action, the child will feel anger and resentment toward you and your partner. Your child will become angry and hostile when they look at what they are missing while on restriction, creating a perception in their mind that you are being unfair and are out to get them. They will begin to feel betrayed by you and will begin to distance themselves from you. Instead of learning from their mistakes they will only learn to be more secretive and not come to you when they are in need. When the punishment is too severe they will lose sight of why they were disciplined and only see you acting as an irrational parent. Your child may develop a fear of you. Having your child fear you is not a desired outcome. If your child fears you and your partner, they will not come to you when faced with peer pressure, drugs, alcohol, sex, etc.

What Is Too Severe?

Obviously the term "severe" is relative and the following examples may seem perfectly appropriate to some, but generally most would agree the following examples of consequences for undesirable behavior are "too severe". An example of a parent being "too severe" is when a child breaks curfew and the parent decides to ground the child for a month. Or when a child does poorly in school and the parent takes away all of the child's privileges. Another severe punishment is when you lose control and hit your child.

When you discipline your child you want the negative behavior to stop. You do not want the behavior to return after one week or a month. You want your child to learn from their mistakes. If your child is not learning and repeats the negative behavior, it is time to reevaluate your discipline techniques.

You also do not want to be too lenient. If you are passive about discipline, your child will learn they can take advantage of you. If the discipline is too lenient your child will not learn from the severity of their actions. They will not have any respect for you or themselves. "Study after study, including those pioneered in Chicago by Grinker (1962) and continued by Offer (1969), attest that healthy, happy, and self reliant adolescents and young adults are the products of stable homes in which both parents give a great deal of time and attention to the children." (Bowlby 2) In my experience, when a child has passive parents they will grow increasingly disrespectful to you and authority figures such as teachers, principals, law enforcement, etc. Most of these children tend to drop out of school, be involved with drugs and alcohol and will most likely have a criminal record.

Between Severe And Lenient
Lies Appropriate Discipline

I cannot emphasize enough that the consequence should relate to your child's actions. If your child repeatedly does the same behavior, even with appropriate consequences, you and your partner should reevaluate the consequences. (See:

Your Child Is Still Defiant! In Chapter 22) Remember the goal of the consequence should teach your child to make more appropriate choices.   Seeking a mental health professional before, during or after exhausting all efforts from my book is fully recommended.

Behind closed doors you can both decide on an appropriate consequence. This is where you work as a team. Remember, it is okay to disagree. If you feel your partner is too severe or too lenient, discuss the concerns you have with that discipline method.   In the heat of a discussion, or argument, it is easy to lose track of the issue. If you lose track of the issue, go back to what behavior you want to extinguish and how that particular consequence will help to extinguish the negative behavior.

These are some questions you and your partner can ask each other:

1. What feelings did your child's behavior emit?
2. Explore why you are feeling that particular feeling. You want to make sure your issues are not going to cloud your judgment.
. Why did you not like your child's behavior? In other words, what did he/she do wrong?
4. What do you hope your child will gain out of your consequence?

5. What consequence will get the result that you would like?

6. Finally, does your consequence seem reasonable for what your child did?

Going through these 6 questions with your partner will enable you to decide on a consequence that is appropriate and provides learning for your child.

Never Let The Child See You Split

No matter how well you and your partner parent together, you will not always agree on the choice of consequence. When you agree to implement a consequence do not undermine your partner by allowing your child to escape their consequence when your partner is not around. If you believe the consequence is inappropriate then discuss it in a place where your child is not present. When you are discussing the point of contention, remember to attack the point and not each other. Raising a child together is difficult and stressful. This is where you and your partner have an advantage over the single parent. You are able to support each other and work together to determine an appropriate consequence for your child.

Consequences Should Fit The Crime

This is so important that it bears repeating: As often as possible implement consequences that relate to the crime. If it is too severe the child will not learn from their mistakes and if it is too lenient the child will not learn responsibility. When both of you have difficulty implementing appropriate consequences, ask yourselves, "What did the child do that was wrong and how can the consequences teach my child to make more appropriate choices next time?" Remember that consequences are used so the child is able to learn from their mistakes to make more appropriate choices next time.

Without Appropriate Discipline, Your Child Will Not Succeed In Life

Hopefully, you and your partner are in agreement that discipline is a necessary tool. It is your responsibility as parents to provide your child with the necessary guidance for your child to succeed in life. "Children need and want parental guidance while being treated with love and respect. Disciplinary rules should not be abstract, complex, or unclear. " (Campbell 205) Discipline is a major factor that will help you and your partner achieve this goal. If you or your partner choose not to discipline your child it could cost them their life. This might seem harsh, but if you have any concerns about the importance of disciplining your child appropriately, then plan a trip to your local prison or your local morgue. Most children who end up in prison or the morgue had parents who were extreme disciplinarians, such as abusive parents, or extremely passive parents. "To people who have grown up in violent homes, violence is not a crisis, but threatened dissolution of the family or imprisonment is. " (Justice and Justice 115) While the choice is still yours and your children are not out of control, make the changes necessary to parent somewhere appropriately in between.

Notes:_____

_____

_____

_____

_____

_____

_____

_____

8 - To Hit Or Not To Hit – What Is The Answer?

He who establishes his argument by noise and command shows that his reason is weak.

Michel de Montaigne

Well if you ask me, a therapist specializing in parent/child relationship issues as well as a parent, I have to say emphatically, NOT TO HIT! Why? There are many reasons why spanking is not an effective disciplinary technique. First, the word discipline comes from the Latin word disciple, which means to teach and that is exactly what you want to do. You want to teach your children to make more responsible choices by providing logical consequences when your child makes the wrong choices. "Physical pain is no longer seen as the means through which children learn appropriate behavior. Instead, more subtle forms of `chastisement' that engage the mind are recommended for self formation." (Larsen 2 9)   Discipline using logical consequences provides a child with the tools needed to promote responsibility, good self esteem and a good relationship between child and parent.

I have heard many people support the use of spanking as a form of discipline. In fact, I have gone many rounds with family members on how spanking is not an effective tool. I have also heard people state the reason many children are having behavioral problems in school is due to parents not spanking. They will also say that parents do not have any control over their children because they do not use corporal punishment.

If you, or your partner, consider using spanking as a disciplinary technique then ask yourself these questions:

1.   What do you think spanking promotes?
2.   What are your reasons for spanking?
.   What do you hope to accomplish?
4.   Were you spanked as a child?
5.   If you were spanked, who did most of the spanking?
6.   What feelings did you have towards the parent who spanked you?

What Do You Think Spanking Promotes?

Spanking is a form of punishment that promotes violence, fear, pain, humiliation and confusion. How? Here is an example. Lets say that you have a child who hits another child. For punishment, you decide to spank your child. You chose to punish your child because hitting someone is wrong. So as a consequence, YOU HIT YOUR CHILD! So now you are condemning violence with violence. You are also teaching your child that it is ok to hit someone younger and smaller. After all, isn't that what you are doing to your child, hitting someone younger and smaller than you? As you can imagine, this can be extremely confusing to your child.

What Are Your Reasons For Spanking?

I had another family member state that timeouts do not work and spankings do. There are various disciplining techniques and if one does not work, there are many more to try. Some techniques are: work detail, early bedtime, no television, no going out with friends and a whole host of others that may be effective forms of discipline for your child before spanking. "Negative punishment may eliminate undesirable behavior for a time, but it does not teach children alternative approaches to solving problems" (Friedman, 1986) If your reason for spanking is to stop the negative behavior, I admit that it typically stops the negative behavior for that moment. But let's examine exactly what you have taught your child.

You have certainly taught them that you do not approve of the negative behavior, but you have also taught them that any remotely similar behavior in the future is to be concealed from the parent. The use of corporal punishment teaches your child to be more secretive so they do not get caught. Your child has learned to fear the spanking, the parent or both instead of learning that the behavior was wrong because of an ethical or moral reason that lead to a logical consequence that fit the crime. Discipline is implemented to teach your child how to behave outside your scope of control. When the fear of spanking is removed, the child has learned that negative behavior is only wrong when the parent becomes aware of the negative behavior. As an adult your child may carry the belief that negative behavior is acceptable behavior as long as you do not get caught. A logical consequence teaches your child how to behave when a similar situation occurs in the future. Your child will consider the logical consequence to their actions whether you are there to implement a spanking or not. Teaching your child right from wrong through the use of logical consequences will provide your child with a moral and ethical basis for the choices they make later in life.

Fear Breeds Uncertainty

A child, who fears you, cannot think clearly about their actions. They will not trust their instincts when the wrong decision will lead to a spanking. Think about how you feel and react when any decision you make may result in pain. How does fear impact your life? Are you afraid to try new things? Do you have poor self confidence? If you were raised in an environment that utilized corporal punishment, think back to when you were a child. Were you afraid of one or both of your parents? Were you afraid to take risks? If you answered yes to any of these questions, do you want your child to feel the same?

Another question to ask yourself is, "Why do you want your child to fear you?" Do you feel using fear is a way of gaining respect? If yes, then, do you respect Saddam Hussein, the Unabomber or terrorists? Hopefully, you do not respect any of these people. So, there must be other ways to gain respect from your children. "Negative punishment destroys the bond of trust and mutual respect between parent and child." (Kersey, 1990) Spanking promotes fear and confusion. If your goal is to stop the negative behavior while your child is in your presence, then corporal punishment will typically work. If your goal is to prevent the negative behavior beyond your scope of control, then spanking is not an effective technique.

Why Parents Use Spanking As A Form Of Discipline

Parenting without spanking is difficult. When faced with the choice of using a logical consequence as opposed to spanking, spanking is the quickest way to stop the undesirable behavior. And make no mistake about it, in most instances the undesirable behavior will stop when you spank. However, you will not accomplish your ultimate goal, which is to teach your child to learn from their mistakes to make more appropriate choices when faced with similar situations in the future.

Does Spanking Establish An Authority Figure?

A client once said that spanking was the way her children would see her as an authority figure. Does that mean that the only way to view someone as an authority is if they hit? Does your boss have to spank you to convey that they have authority over you? Does your child's teacher or principal have to spank your children in order to convey authority? Hopefully, you have answered, "No." to each of these questions. Then, why do you have to spank in order to gain authority? The truth of the matter is that spanking only conveys that you have lost control for that moment. If you want your child to respect you and see you as an authority figure, teach them how to stay in control of a situation. Teach them behavior that you would like them to emulate.

What If Spanking Does Not Work?

What do you try next? Spank harder next time. If you are going to use spanking as a form of discipline, use it as a last possible resort or you may find yourself left with nowhere to go if it does not work. Believe me when I tell you, sometimes spanking does not work, especially in children who respond well to other forms of discipline. My son is a perfect example of a child who learns best when I tell him what he did wrong and why a favorite toy, television show, dessert or activity is taken away. My daughter, on the other hand, could be described as feisty. She would be a prime candidate for a spanking if we believed in using that form of punishment. She repeatedly fought against our rules as a baby. Harsh words, removal of a favorite toy or activity, timeouts, isolation in the crib in her room for a few minutes did not appear to work. But we were diligent and after bouncing ideas off each other, we eventually came to the conclusion that this was her personality: stubborn. So we were consistent in our efforts until the undesirable behavior slowly and eventually diminished down to a manageable level. My husband and I are just aware of the fact that our daughter requires more thought and effort to teach her what we view as acceptable behavior.

If you reach the point where you are feeling frustrated and enraged to the point where you feel the need to spank your child, you have lost control. But you now have a child who does not respond to your primary discipline technique. Your child has learned the power of "pushing your buttons" and will use this knowledge to control you and your emotions.

How Do You Learn Best?

Some of us prefer lecture, some prefer group discussions, some prefer video, interactive CD ROMs, books, audiotapes, etc. Children learn in the same way. Understanding what works best for your child and using discipline techniques that are appropriate for your unique child is the key to effectively teaching your child the rules of your household. Also keep in mind that the rules for your household are probably different than the rules for your grandparents and siblings. And the rules for your religion, your race, your city, your state, and your country are different than others. So when you use logical consequences to teach your child, you are also teaching your child how to behave appropriately outside your home. Faced with unfamiliar surroundings, your child will reason logical consequences to their actions.

Were You Or Your Partner Spanked As A Child?

If you answered yes, which most of you probably were, think back to what you learned from that experience. Now you might say, "I was spanked and I turned out fine." And for all intentional purposes, you might be a great person despite the spankings or you might say, "because of the spankings" if you are in favor of corporal punishment. In today's society we are more knowledgeable about parenting techniques. There are more books, research and statistics available today than ever before and the beauty of this research is that it is becoming more easily acquired with the invention of the internet. Use the internet to further educate yourself about the use of spanking. Type in "spanking" on your favorite search engine and read some of the findings yourself. You can find a list of websites regarding spanking at the end of this chapter. Most are obviously against spanking, but some do advocate the use of spanking under certain very specific circumstances.

Stop Driving An Outdated Model

Think back to your family car when you were young. Why are you not driving in the same car? Most likely, your parents traded it in for a new car years ago. The car manufacturer has either discontinued that model or has made improvements to fit the needs of today's society. You can apply the same reasoning to parenting techniques. The techniques your parents used might have been fine when you were a child but now with new technology it is outdated and needs to be redefined. It is time to use your newly acquired knowledge from my book and other psychotherapists and Psychologists who do not advocate the use of corporal punishment and change with the times.

Who Did Most Of The Spanking In Your House?

Explore who did most of the punishment in your house. Did you live in a house where your mother said, "Wait until your father comes home."? If so, what kind of feelings did that evoke. I would imagine that you began to fear your father or the parent who executed the spankings. In most instances that feeling of fear made you distant from your father or the parent who executed the spankings. You were probably afraid to tell your parents about important issues that required their guidance. Is that the type of relationship you want with your child? Do you want your child to fear you and be afraid to come to you? Continuing to spank your child will evoke feelings of fear and they will turn to others for guidance. If you want a relationship with your child where your child feels comfortable to approach you with difficult topics such as drugs or sex, then you will need to utilize a disciplining technique that your children will respect, but not fear.

You Completely Disagree With Me, Then Follow These Rules

If you completely disagree with me on the issue of spanking and you will continue to use it as a disciplinary technique, then at least follow the guidelines for using corporal punishment outlined in a reprint of a debate over the use of corporal punishment where Robert E. Larzelere outlines a set of rules when using corporal punishment. The guidelines go into more detail in the article, but essentially it says to only use spankings on children between the ages of two to six years and only as a last resort. You are to administer the spanking with an open hand, no spoons, paddles, belts, or object of any kind, and use only one, no more than two, quick smacks on the bottom. If you do not use it as an absolute last resort or you use an object or hit more than twice or excessively hard, then you are unequivocally abusing your child. Every case study and every rational psychotherapist who has reviewed the case studies agrees that the use of corporal punishment in any way other than the guidelines for using corporal punishment outlined by

Lazalere is considered abuse and a large majority of psychotherapists, I am one of them, believe the use of corporal punishment even under these circumstances would be abuse as well. According to the same study from which these guidelines were created, spankings administered in this way did not appear to have significant long or short term harm on the child. But the same research also revealed that the use of spankings in this manner was equally effective as using non corporal punishment discipline techniques. (Mason, 1994) Knowing that the effectiveness of using corporal punishment or using other forms of discipline is equally effective, how anyone would continue to use corporal punishment in the disciplining of their child is beyond me. I offer these guidelines to minimize the harm to your child should you decide to administer corporal punishment despite my best efforts to convince you otherwise.

Others Who Agree With Me

If you are not convinced about the negative effects spanking has on your child, here are some other professional opinions about the subject. As websites can change addresses or locations, some of these sites may not exist at the time you look for them on the internet. If you are unable to locate these sites, type in a keyword search for "spanking".

You will find an abundance of information regarding the use of corporal punishment

http://www.religioustolerance.org/spankin2.htm
Drs. T. Berry Brazelton, Penelope Leach, and Benjamin Spock, probably the most influential child psychologists and pediatricians, all recommend against spanking. So does the American Psychological Association and the National Association of Social Workers.

http://www.aap.org/research/ps 8exs1.htm
Current Practices Regarding Counseling on Discipline When counseling parents on disciplining their child, nearly all pediatricians recommend parents use positive reinforcement of good behavior (99.1%) and non physical methods of punishment for negative behavior, such as time out or removal of privileges (9 .8%).

http://silcon.com/~ptave/bradshaw.htm
"...People who justify physical punishment were almost always spanked and physically punished themselves . . .. When grown ups, who were spanked,

spank their own children, they are activating their unconscious need to pass the humiliation on."

http://www.bconnex.net/~cspcc/empathic_parenting/spank.htm

"Maybe you will say that spanking children is different because it's in the family and therefore part of a relationship which is both loving and stressful. But that would make it perfectly alright for your partner to end arguments with you by giving you a good slap."

http://www.naturalchild.com/jan_hunt/tenreasons.html

"A punished child becomes preoccupied with feelings of anger and fantasies of revenge, and is thus deprived of the opportunity to learn more effective methods of solving the problem at hand. Thus, a punished child learns little about how to handle or prevent similar situations in the future."

Parent Together Without Spanking

The goal of this book is to educate you on the importance of disciplining together. If you are in a situation where you are trying to convince your partner not to use corporal punishment, do not try to engage them on your own. Trying to convince a person who believes in spanking is difficult. You want to present them with the most convincing argument available. Ask them to read this chapter of my book. Tell them that you are convinced of the need to not spank and you would prefer they do not spank until they have read this chapter.

Whether your partner ultimately reads my book or not, agrees with me or not, parenting together only works when you LISTEN to your partner. It is important that your partner feels heard. After listening, you can express your concerns and ideas in a CALM tone. If you feel the conversation is getting heated, take a break and address the issue at another time. Remember that both of you are on the same team and have the same goal to raise a responsible, respectful, courageous and high self esteem child. The way to achieve this goal is to work as a team and decide the best parenting techniques to obtain this goal. I hope your parenting moves forward without the use of corporal punishment so your child can have the best possible childhood and potential for a successful adult life.

Notes:_____

_____

_____

_____

_____

_____

_____

_____

_____

9 - The Cycle Of Abuse

Those who do not remember the past are condemned to repeat it.

George Santayana

This Dad's Childhood

I had a mixed bag of some good, but mostly bad memories as a young child. I was a latchkey kid when I was young, coming home to an empty house most days. I would watch a lot of television in my house with a friend from down the street until someone came home. At night, when both my parents were home, I remember a great deal of silence or television. As an only child I played a lot in my room, alone. But I also remember playing organized baseball, football and basketball at the local park. My father was the coach, or assistant coach, on most of the teams. Those are mostly good memories. I lived in a predominantly Hispanic neighborhood until the age of twelve when my father moved us into a predominantly white middle class area. All but one of my relatives lived on the east coast. My grandmother on my father's side lived in Northern California. I did not have any brothers, sisters, cousins, uncles, aunts, and grandparents even remotely close to me, geographically or otherwise. My mother and father were strangers living in the same house. As I grew older I became another stranger in a house of strangers. About the age of twelve, my father buried himself in his work and admitted to me when I was older that he abandoned me to be raised exclusively by my mother who did not have a clue how to raise a teenager. I enjoyed playing tennis and basketball and, looking back, I believe a played a great deal of tennis and basketball to escape my dysfunctional home life. My parents divorced when I was sixteen. I broke off contact with my mother almost immediately after she moved out of the house, but I maintained contact with my father primarily due to my inability to financially support myself. My father remarried and moved in with his new wife and I was kicked out of my house to live on the street for about a year. I had a lot of issues that took years of self examination, time, meeting my wife and eventually having my children to heal most of the wounds of the past. To say my wife and I came from different childhood backgrounds would be an understatement.

This Mom's Childhood

I did not come from an abusive environment and have no direct experience with abuse. My husband, on the other hand, sadly came from a neglectful environment and can give more insight into the feelings associated with living in that type of environment. Working in the foster care system and in my private practice, I have dealt with issues of both physical and emotional abuse far too often. When I was new to the field, dealing with issues of abuse proved to be challenging and uncomfortable, but through many years of experience and education, I know far too well the subject of abuse and can say confidently that I know how to help the abused and the perpetrators of abuse.

Survivors Of Abuse

"Parents do not 'own' their children but are responsible for promoting their well being, which means providing a home free of abuse. " (Justice and Justice 1 5) If you are a survivor of abuse you have probably noticed that you have come from a long line of generations that have been abused. I am sure you would like to prevent the cycle of abuse to your children. I am also sure that the abusers in your family did not want to pass it down to you either. So how do you, after generations of abuse, stop the cycle?

Individual Therapy For Victims Of Abuse

The first step is to seek individual therapy so you are able to work on issues of abuse. Psychotherapists, like myself, have experience with issues of abuse and have the education to know how to prevent the cycle of abuse from being passed down to your children. I also suggest parenting classes.

If you were a victim of abuse you would definitely want to share this with your partner. You also want to learn from your partner the type of environment they knew as a child. Hopefully, if it was a healthy environment, your partner will be able to help teach you how to provide a more supportive, loving and nurturing home.

Parenting Classes For Victims Of Abuse

"For many, only the threat or actual removal of the children from the family or the threat of imprisonment are sufficient coercion for abusive parents to seek therapy." (Justice and Justice 116) You are a product of your environment. Does this mean you will be an abuser? Not necessarily, but the cards are stacked against you. We learn what we live. My husband does not want to fall into old family patterns with our children. Fortunately he has worked through a lot of his issues through self exploration and education about mental and emotional abuse long before we met. That was one of the aspects of his personality that drew me to him. He seemed to have an understanding of his tortured past and a sense that he wanted a better life for himself and eventually his children. He has said to me that having children is like therapy for him. When he disciplines or communicates with our children in a way that his parents would never have done, he feels sadness for the child he once was who had to endure emotional and mental abuse and happiness for our children who will never know what that abuse was like. With each passing day he reestablishes new patterns while discarding the old one's, growing more and more distant from the old familiar family patterns.

If you are a parent who was raised in a primarily Reasonable Parenting environment and your partner was not, agreeing to attend parenting classes together is another terrific way to discover how to parent together. Parenting classes can benefit the parent who grew up in an abusive environment as well as a person who grew up in a nurturing and loving family. If you have entered into a relationship where both of you have a history of abuse, it would be extremely beneficial for both of you to take parenting classes. By participating in a local parenting group, you and your partner can learn new and more effective ways to raise your child. It also offers you the opportunity to meet other parents who are having the same concerns and struggles.

When choosing a class, be sure the material fits your family's current situation. You do not want a class that primarily discusses middle school age child issues when your child is in high school. Find a group that covers your particular situation. For example, if your family were facing discipline problems with your teenager, then finding a group covering how to effectively discipline a teenage child would be ideal. If finding a group with this particular issue proves to be difficult, then finding a group dealing with out of control kids would be the next best option. Also be sure the group provides a comfortable, non judgmental and safe environment.

Notes:_____

_____

_____

_____

_____

_____

_____

_____

_____

10 - Connect With Your Child

I define joy as a sustained sense of well-being and internal peace
- a connection to what matters.

Oprah Winfrey

When you and you partner first met, you shared your interests to learn more about your partner's likes and dislikes. If you only discussed controversial issues that evoked heated arguments, you probably would not have continued your relationship. The same is true for your child. Continuous heated arguments with your child about their behavior will break down your relationship with your child. Find new ways to connect or reconnect with your child. Go to a movie, listen and find interests in your child's music, television shows or activities. You and your partner are spending quality time with your child. Do not talk about any issues that might elicit controversy. Your goal is to regain a positive relationship with your child: Discipline can wait! When you must discipline your child in the future, your child will be more receptive. You should see a decrease in your child's undesirable behavior.

Although the suggestion above should provide some benefit to your relationship with your child, below I provide some other specific techniques for redirecting their negative behavior.

Breaking Down Your Child's Defenses

When children play games, especially therapeutic games, their walls, or defenses, break down. This is your opportunity to learn about your child's perceptions of the world, their friends, siblings, grandparents and you. After reading and playing the therapeutic games in "Good Parents Bad Parenting", your relationship with your child will forever be changed and you will have a greater understanding of how to parent your child together.

Redirection

When you see a situation that will result in undesirable behavior, redirect your child into another activity. This technique can be done with or without your child's knowledge. If your child shows a consistent pattern of not behaving appropriately in a specific location or with another child, remove your child from the environment that is creating the misbehavior. Only reintroduce your child into that environment when you feel confident your child will act appropriately. Obviously this technique is easier to implement on young children. For teenagers who are having difficulty with a specific friend or location, the technique can be utilized, but it is difficult to monitor.

Direct Communication

An overused and abused technique for conveying information to your child is through direct communication. Too often parents use this form of communication as their primary and exclusive form of conveying information, thereby dissipating its effect. Direct communication should be used when the moment is one of critical importance to you, your partner, or your child and the situation clearly dictates the use of direct communication. Personal safety issues involving drugs, sex, alcohol or dangerous activities are situations where this approach should be utilized.

Opportunity

Opportunity is the third form of conveying information to your child that can be very effective. Remember when you tried to teach your child something they absolutely did not want to learn. The harder you push the information, the less they learn. For example, teaching your child about elephants from a book is less effective than taking your child to the zoo. Create opportunities to make learning easier. In your daily life, take advantage of opportunities that allow you to teach your child desirable behavior when you see desirable behavior in others. Good manners, proper etiquette, consideration of others, fairness are taught by using other children's behavior as a model. You are not telling your child to behave; you are teaching your child good behavior by using a third party example in the real world.

Notes:_____

_____

_____

_____

_____

_____

_____

_____

11 - Grand Parenting   Redefining Your Parent's Role

The reason grandparents and grandchildren get along so well is that they have a common enemy.

Sam Levenson

You and your spouse can discuss how much you want the grandparents to be involved in your child's life. If you grew up in a healthy relationship with your parents, then naturally you want them to be a part of your new family. If you grew up in an unhealthy relationship then perhaps limited or no exposure is something to be discussed, depending upon the present relationship you or your partner have with them. Your spouse is your family now and your spouse's feelings must be considered your highest priority and consideration.

According to Cherlin and Furstenberg, "The New American Grandparent: A Place in the Family, a Life Apart", most grandparents they interviewed generally accepted their new role as a loving companion to their grandchildren with the parenting left to their children. But even if you come from the healthiest family background, your parents and in laws at one time or another will disagree with how you are raising your child. They will feel you are too passive or too strict in general or specific instances. They will determine your overall parenting style based on the time you spend with them in the presence of your children, which is a completely different parenting dynamic to judge someone's ability to parent.

Try to remember that your parents are from a different generation where the rules, education and parental experience were different. It is only natural, through the course of time, a greater understanding and analysis of parenting combined with improved methods of dispersing this information to the public has provided the younger generation with access to a greater amount of parenting knowledge. Keep in mind that grandparents do have more experience. With this experience comes a more critical eye. I have no doubt when my children are having children, I will be critical of their parenting abilities as well. I may have to reread this paragraph when I am a grandparent to remind myself how I viewed grandparents when I was parenting my children. I do not recommend you discuss this topic with your parents unless you want to start an argument.

The bottom line is that you and your spouse are in charge of the discipline. As long as your discipline style is not threatening, punitive, degrading or illegal, trust your instincts to parent. If you are having a battle with your parents, assure them you and your spouse appreciate their input but you have the final say on the way you discipline your children. Try to keep in mind that their over involvement is a sign that they care about the well being of your child. A parent that rarely sees your child and never offers any advice does not have your child's best interest at heart. If your parents continue to interfere despite your efforts to set reasonable limits on their involvement, remind them that this is their time to enjoy being grandparents and leave the discipline to you and your spouse.

You must gain the support of your spouse, especially where grandparents are involved. With your spouses support, you are never alone in the success or failure of your parenting decisions. With your spouse's support, you are more likely to make appropriate parenting decision and you are more likely to keep the grandparent's opinions about your parenting abilities in their proper perspective. Remember that your spouse and your children are your responsibility. This is the time in your life when you learn you are not a little kid anymore. You are a responsible adult. Parents can often make you feel like a child no matter how hold you are. If you have a difficult time expressing your feelings to your parents, find a small tangible object to hold while you speak with your parents about parenting issues. That object will serve to remind you that you are no longer a child; a picture of your wedding, your wedding ring, your car keys, your wallet, anything that gives you courage to stand your ground. The goal is to convey to your parents that you are not a child anymore and you deserve the space required to raise your child the way you and your spouse decide. Parents often view their children as the little boy or girl who once could not tie their own shoes, dress themselves or take proper care of the family pet and forget you are not a child anymore. You paid your dues as a child, you are married, have a child and now it is time for you to be an adult!

Notes:_____

_____

_____

_____

_____

12 - The Divorced Parent

We have met the enemy and it is us.

Walt Kelly

In their research on the consequences of single parenthood, McLanahan and Sandefur (1994) found that growing up with just one biological parent approximately doubles the risk of dropping out of high school, from approximately 15% in two parent households (defined as households with two biological parents) to about 0% in one parent households (defined as households in which one biological parent is absent). The same study also shows a decrease in overall test scores for children of single parent households. Obviously these statistics illustrate the horrible effects divorce can have on a child, but remaining together for the sake of the children can be equally damaging. "The type of adjustment problems in children associated with marital conflict and with divorce are similar, with the largest effects obtained with externalizing disorders, lack of self regulation, low social responsibility, and cognitive agency, and to a lesser extent with internalizing, social agency, and self esteem." (Hetherington 95) When you and your partner ultimately chose divorce as the best option, the transition is extremely difficult for everyone. Typically the mother receives primary custody of the child, but whether the child lives with the mother or the father, becoming a single parent can be draining, stressful and exhausting. The best advice I can give a single parent is to find a good team of people for support. This support network can help give you some required space and relaxation. It can also restore your energy so you can be the best parent you can be.

The ideal support would come from your own family. If you live close to your parents or have siblings, they can help by watching the child to allow you to take time for yourself. If you are not fortunate to live near your family, you can find people in your church or befriend other divorced people. You can trade services with these people. They might be able to baby sit one night and you can watch their children another night. No matter who makes up your support network, the goal is for you to feel that you are not alone. Being a single parent can be overwhelming, stressful and tiring. Having a group of people to help can give you the time you need to regroup and reenergize yourself which will allow you to be a better parent.

One of the most challenging aspects of the divorce is to continue to parent your child together. "At the present time, available evidence suggests that parental conflict may prove to be one critical mediating variable affecting the post divorce adjustment of children." (Forehand, Long and Brody 156) Remember, even though the two of you have ended your marriage, you are both your child's parents for life. Because of this, you will be forever connected. In the ideal divorce, both of you will agree on the same disciplinary techniques as well as providing the same structure and consequences. Try to remember the importance of maintaining a healthy father/son relationship for your child's future. "Father absence approximately doubles the risk of dropping out of school regardless of a young person's race or ethnicity." (McLanahan and Teitler 88) Unfortunately many divorced parents do not agree, especially when their children are involved. So, how do you work together to provide the guidance, structure and nurturing environment your child needs to succeed in life? Here are a few steps to help you tackle this difficult dilemma.

1. Do not engage in the power struggle when your child says, "Well Dad lets me." Or "Mom said I could."

2. Learn to let non life threatening issues lie. Examples of this would be: a later bedtime, staying out later, not doing homework right after school, no chores, eating too much junk food, etc. This point is important because if you don't let these issues lie, you will often find yourself in a continuous and stressful battle with your Ex. You and your Ex have different ways of handling situations and as long as your child's safety and necessities are not in jeopardy, it is much easier to let these issues lie rather than battling over them. The child will also benefit by not having both parents argue all the time. It is much easier for a child to adapt to each parents sets of rules than it is to deal with both parents fighting and putting the child in the middle.

. Teach your child that different sets of rules exist at each parent's house and what your child can do at one house might not be acceptable at the other parent's house.

4. Never speak negatively about the other parent to your child. Sometimes this may be difficult when you feel enraged about their behavior, but your child loves both parents. When you speak negatively about your Ex, it puts the child in a position where they have to take sides and choose one parent over the other.

Your child also does not have to hear about all your dirty laundry. It will only add stress and anxiety to an already stressful situation.

5. Try to be the mature parent and talk to the other parent if there is a disagreement. Do not degrade or blame the other parent no matter how wrong you feel they are. Remember to let them hear your point in an appropriate way. (See: Agree To Disagree in Establishing The Rules in Chapter 2)

6. Never put your child in the middle. You and your spouse are your child's parents forever. You and your spouse made the decision to have a child and you and your spouse made the decision to divorce, not your child. It is unfair and can cause your child emotional stress if they feel they need to take sides. They love you both and it is not their fight.

If you follow these 6 steps you are on your way to becoming a better parent with your Ex. Remember that you are divorced for a reason and you will not agree on everything. If you still get along, you would probably still be married!

Depending on the circumstances of the divorce, there might be feelings of hostility, resentment, betrayal or anger. These feelings tend to linger for a long time after the divorce.

However, dealing with your issues in a positive way teaches your child the appropriate way to interact with difficult people. At one time in your life you and your Ex loved each other enough to create a child. You owe it to your child to act peaceful and civilized to the parent that played a role in creating your child.

Just remember that your child will have an easier time adapting to environments with different sets of rules as long as the environments are consistent. Both environments need not have the same rules, which obviously would be the ideal but is unrealistic. As long your child knows what is expected in both homes, your child will be able to adjust to each set of rules.

Stop Acting Like Children

Now that you know how easy the transition can be, why is it hard to implement these changes? The goal of divorce is to hopefully provide happiness for you and your children. This is a time to let go of your disappointments and frustrations to begin the healing process. The first step to making your divorce work is to let go of the anger. Remember the reason or reasons you divorced. It was probably a consequence of many choices that both of you made. You tried many different interventions to help keep your marriage together with little, or no, success. Once you are able to let go of the anger and sadness, you will be in a better position to work with your ex. The key to making your divorce a success is to learn new coping skills. You are divorced for a reason and most likely it was because you and your spouse were not happy. This is the time in your life where you can make changes and not fall into the same patterns that drove you to divorce. Teach your children how to interact with someone appropriately even if you disagree with them. Remember that your children are looking to you and your ex for guidance and support. The more anger and hostility you show to your ex the more angry and hostile your children will be to you, your spouse, siblings, friends and acquaintances. Show your children that something good resulted from your divorce. Show your children that the fighting and arguing is over now that you are not living together. Resist the temptation to push each other's buttons. If you feel frustrated and angry with your ex focus on the positive result from your divorce; you are not married to your ex anymore!

Your child is the innocent bystander of the divorce. They rely on both parents to love them and take care of them in a safe, nurturing and supportive environment You can divorce your spouse but your child cannot divorce their parents. Taking that into consideration, if your child sees that you and your spouse can communicate appropriate and both care for the child's well being without getting into power struggles, you and your ex will emotionally help your child through this difficult transition.

Children Blame Themselves

When a child goes through a divorce, they often feel it was their fault. The child feels if they had behaved appropriately more often or if they had just done something different, then their parents would still be together. You and your ex will be able to address these issues with your child in an appropriate way. With you and your ex comforting your child on these issues, they will begin to understand that they did not cause the divorce. Even if you think your child is adjusting well to the divorce, constantly check in with them. When you talk to your child remind them why you and your Ex needed to divorce. In my private practice many children say they do not know why their parents needed to divorce even after their parents told them numerous times. The children may have blocked it out or found the conversation too difficult to hear. It has also been my experience that children do not ask questions about their parent's divorce. Avoiding the topic is their way of coping with unpleasant emotions. It is perfectly appropriate for you to broach the topic. When you speak with your child, remind your child that they are safe and loved along with constant reassurance that the divorce was not because they did anything wrong. Express your reasons for the divorce in factual form, using age appropriate language and do not assign blame. Avoid details when explaining the necessity for your divorce. You can be general about the situation by saying, "Sometimes parents can't live together anymore due to a lot of fighting and arguing. As a result you and your spouse weren't happy living together anymore." Children need to know the reasons for the divorce but also need reassurance that they are loved and will be cared for after the divorce. Another wonderful way to convey your devotion to your child is to tell your child, "Parents divorce each other but do not divorce their children." Another approach is to point out the positive aspects of your divorce. You can explain that you and your partner won't be fighting anymore. You could also let them know they will have two birthdays and two Christmas/Hanukah celebrations, resulting in more presents! If your child is living with a stepparent, reassure your child that both of you will always be there. "Frequent visits from the nonresidential parent could reduce children's fears that the stepparent is a parent replacement resulting in more positive stepparent stepchild relationships and better outcomes for children." (Hetherington 00)

Children often have a difficult time expressing their feelings about divorce for fear of upsetting their parents. A non threatening way to allow your child to express their feelings can be through a game. Your child can become lost in the fun of the game, which will allow your child to express their true feelings about your divorce. Here is a game I created to help facilitate their expression of emotions:

Expressing Feelings About Divorce Game

You will need:
Poster Board
1 die
Game pieces/coins
Markers

Draw an outline of a house on a poster board size piece of paper. Along the inside of your drawn outline, draw a pathway of squares that eventually connect to allow continuous play. Your squares should be big enough to write the questions below. Make sure you include a start square. You do not need an end square because there are no losers in this game. In addition to the following questions add any questions you feel are important for your situation.

Questions For The Game:

How do you feel about your parents divorce?

Why did you/your parents get a divorce?

What do you miss about your parents being together?

What are you afraid of?

What makes you sad about the divorce?

Same something positive about the divorce

Do you think the divorce is your fault? Why? Why not?

What do you like to do with your mother/child?

What do you like to do with your father/child?

What do you dream about?

Do you want your parents to get back together? Why? Why not?

What can you do to make yourself happy?

What can you do if you're angry?

What do you like to do at your mom's house?

What do you like to do at your dad's house?

What don't you like about your parents divorce?

To Play:

Roll the die and move your game piece accordingly. The game is over when you feel your child's concerns and feelings about the divorce are addressed. This game allows your child to express their feelings in a safe and nurturing environment.

Notes:_____

_____

_____

_____

_____

_____

_____

_____

_____

13 - Parenting Someone Else's Child

*Without a sense of caring,
there can be no sense of community.*

Anthony J. D'Angelo

Parenting someone else's child has to be one of the toughest challenges in parenting. Throughout my years in grad school, all therapists learn that biological parents should discipline their child. For years I told my clients to allow the birth parent to do all the disciplining. However, this created problems when the birth parent was at work and the stepparent was home with the stepchild. Many clients would express frustration when their own children would receive consequences but their stepsibling would not. The ideal world would have you, your spouse and your spouses ex work as a team to equally administer logical consequences. Unfortunately we do not live in an ideal world. So how can you discipline a child who is not yours?

Defining Your Roles

First you and your spouse, boyfriend, girlfriend or significant other must discuss what role is expected from each of you. Does your partner want you to discipline your stepchild and do you object to implementing the consequences? What role are you comfortable playing hands off, equal partner, report taker or total disciplinarian.

1. The "Hands–Off" parent does not intervene and does not discipline the child. They might offer support to their partner as well as to the child. The "hands off" parent can discuss their concerns with their partner, but the biological parent implements the discipline techniques.

2. The next style is the "Equal Partner". This parent provides the discipline and consequence and treats the stepchild like their biological child. The stepparent and biological parent discuss appropriate disciplinary techniques and both feel free to implement the consequences.

. The "Report Taker" parent does not provide any discipline but takes notes of the child's behavior throughout the day and reports back to the biological parent. Again this parent does not directly discipline the child.

4. The "Total Disciplinarian" parent is basically raising the stepchild. The biological parent can feel guilty for the divorce or is at work the entire day and does not provide any of the discipline. The biological parent does not discuss disciplinary techniques with the stepparent. In this situation the stepparent provides the discipline and consequence to all the children.

Are you both comfortable with your new roles and responsibilities? If these new roles create problems for either of you, or the household, then both of you might need to reevaluate your choice of roles and discuss a new plan. Each of you should answer the following questions openly and honestly to be sure one parent does not feel any apprehension toward their role in the family.

1. Does your partner agree with your role?
2. Is your role creating conflict?
. Are you happy with your role?
4. Is your partner happy with your role?
5. Is it working?

If you answered, "NO" to #'s 1, , 4 and 5 and "YES" to #2, you and your partner need to find new roles in the family. Instead of having conflict with the same routine, find a new solution to the situation. With your patience, creativity and joint effort you can make this work.

Assessing The Child

Being a parent to someone else's child requires a tremendous amount of understanding. Remember, the child you are parenting has come from a broken home. Most children of divorce have a fantasy that their mother and father will get back together and you are in the way of that fantasy coming true. A child of divorce often has anger issues, abandonment, guilt, sadness and an abundance of other negative feelings.

"Stepfamilies that weather the initial challenges of family formation tend to be those that recognize that building a sense of family takes time, family boundaries must be flexible to accommodate existing ties to noncustodial parents and extended family, and stepparents cannot replace biological parents and may need to develop a separate, nontraditional parenting role." (McLanahan and Teitler 1 9) Here you are, a divorced parent who is remarried to another divorced parent and now has a child with your new spouse. Oh, the family dynamics! In between transferring children to their other parents' houses, raising a new child and incorporating your blended family, how do you and your spouse have time to enjoy your relationship?

The best way to reduce the chaos is to work on making your home as consistent as possible. Your children and your spouse's children will most likely have a different set of rules when they are living at their other parent's houses. You are not in control of the rules implemented at the Ex's homes so learn to let things go. However, you and your spouse are in control of the rules that are enforced at your home. The more consistent you implement your house rules, the more secure your children will feel. All the children are adjusting to new parents, new siblings and a new living environment. Their world has been turned upside down. Do not expect everyone to get along and love each other. You chose your spouse. Your children did not choose your spouse or their children.

Family Meetings

To make the transition run as smoothly as possible, you and your spouse can implement family meetings. In these meetings you and your spouse should allow all the children to express their feelings and concerns. In these meetings you and your spouse can reinforce rules, consequences, expectations, etc. It is also a place where your children can provide input and recommendations. Remember that the goal of the meeting is to create a safe, nurturing and stable environment for your new family.

Everyone should feel free to express their feelings, which will allow every member to play a big part in the new family. This should allow your blended family to be on the road to a successful new, larger, blended family.

Family Meeting Example:

Step One:

> Two days before the family meeting, on the refrigerator hang a piece of paper up with numbers 1 10. Write a note on top for all family members to write down issues they would like to be addressed at the family meeting. You can put subcategories such as chores, vacation, rules, etc.

Step Two:

> Get everyone involved in setting up the family meeting. Have one member in charge of setting up the room, have another member or members in charge of snacks, etc. The more you have them involved in the preparation the more they will be involved in the meeting.

Step Three:

> Make sure everyone is present and on time and most of all, make sure you and your partner are ready and eager to participate in the meeting equally.

Step Four:

> Make sure all family members issues have been addressed and that all members have had an equal say in the meeting.

Step Five:

> Schedule another meeting and make an agenda for topics that will be addressed in the next meeting. Before everyone leaves make sure that all members understand the issues that were addressed in the meeting.

Learn From The Past

Another important part to making your blended family a success is to communicate with your spouse. You do not want to repeat the same mistakes you made with your Ex. Learn from the past and incorporate it into your new marriage. You also want to make sure you and your spouse spend alone time together. Being part of a blended family can be very stressful. You and your spouse will need to work together as a team and remember to take time to be a couple.

If your blended family is having a difficult time with the transition, look into attending a local support group. A support group can help your family learn techniques to make the adjustment a more positive experience.

Suggestions For Success

1. Spend alone time with your spouse
2. Provide new family traditions
. Listen to the children
4. Allow each child to get 15 minutes of alone time with you and or your spouse
5. Include children in discussions that concern the family
6. Provide a consistent, structured environment
. Provide family meetings
8. Go on family outings with all the children
9. Treat all children equally and fairly. (Adjusting for age when appropriate)
10. Provide children with their own space so they can have some alone time
11. Do not say bad things about your Ex or your spouse's Ex.
12. Be sensitive to the children's feelings and concerns
1 . Do not take over the role as their mother or father. They didn't die; they are just not living with you
14. Respect them and their parent, and then they will respect you

Notes:_____

_____

_____

_____

_____

_____

_____

_____

_____

14 - When Your Child Does Not Meet Your Expectations

The greatest loss of time is delay and expectation, which depend upon the future. We let go the present, which we have in our power, and look forward to that which depends upon chance, and so relinquish a certainty for an uncertainty.

Seneca

When you and your partner were expecting your first child, you probably enjoyed mapping out their entire future. If you are raising a girl, you may have envisioned her as the first female president or a ballerina or a doctor. If you are raising a boy, you may have imagined him as a famous athlete or the president or a lawyer or doctor. If these were not your child's goals, you probably had other goals equally as grand. After some time with your child, you may have realized that your son was not as athletic as you had hoped. He may be a sensitive child, enjoying arts and crafts and listening to music.

Or you realized your daughter was not the smartest child in her class and was as graceful as an ox. At some point in their development, you began to realize your goals for your child were not going to happen. As parents, we hold on to these dreams until we realize that our child has dreams of their own or has no interest or talent for the dreams we envisioned for them.

During a Mommy And Me class I observed many parents creating beautiful art projects for their children. Not only would they complete the project, they would discourage their child from touching the art project at all! The sad, yet strangely hysterical, point worth noting about my observations was that the parents wrote their child's name and date on the completed art project. This was not the child's project: it was the parents. A few months into the class, I observed these same children doing everything but art during art time. The children learned they could not work on their own art project and if they tried to participate, they were directed to create what their parents envisioned. Many of the children did not enjoy creating art and the parents could not understand why. They never realized how their actions created their child's disinterest. Their child felt discouraged and inadequate because their mothers never let them create their own art projects.

Stop Harming Your Child's Self Esteem

I hope this is the only time when these mothers will not allow their child to build their own self esteem, but chances are this pattern will continue. If you see yourself as one of these parents, know you are harming your child's self esteem and your child's ability to perform activities on their own. If you allow your child to experiment with different activities and enjoy the process of their own discovery, you will begin to see your child for who they are. Instead of forcing your dreams on your child, you will enjoy experiencing your child's dreams.

The parents that allow their child to do the art projects raise a child that looks forward to art. These parents share in the pleasure of their child's development and exploration. The more you and your partner step back and watch your child learn and develop, the more you will see exactly where their interests and potential lie. With a clear understanding of your child's strengths and weaknesses, you can then direct your child into activities that maximize their strengths and minimize their weaknesses while increasing their self esteem. Your child might not be the first female president or the famous football player, but they will feel your support and love no matter where their art projects, and their dreams, take them.

You Are Enlightened, But Your Spouse Is Not

How do you approach a partner who may be placing undue pressure on your child and your child has a difficult time living up to that expectation? As is expressed throughout this book, you must communicate your concerns with your partner. My recommendations for approaching your partner regarding this very important issue is to not place blame or cast judgment on your partner. It is important that you approach this subject matter in a very positive way. Instead of explaining what your partner might be doing wrong with your child, turn it around and say things that you admire about your partner's relationship with your child. Then I would continue on that wavelength and add what aspects of the relationship you would like to see more of. You could also ask your partner what he/she enjoys about the relationship as well as how he/she could improve the relationship with his/her child. The more positive you are with this delicate situation the more positive your results will be. Remember that nobody wants to feel that they are creating harm to their child. If you present this issue in an attacking or blaming manner, your partner can often feel like he/she has to defend his/her relationship and therefore, it will only add friction to the relationship instead of improving it.

The Death Of A Dream

What do you do when your partner wants your child to be that super athlete, movie star, singer, or Nobel Prize winning scientist and yet your child shows no interest in any of your partner's dreams. Or perhaps your child shows an interest in being a famous athlete but is born with two left feet. The difficulty comes when you try to communicate your disappointments in the loss of the ideal child, or dream, to your partner. As parents, we often place our expectations on our child because we did not fulfill our own expectations. Parents who fully pursue and achieve their dreams, generally do not pressure their child to pursue the same dream. They strangely almost discourage their child from following in their footsteps. Perhaps your partner wanted to be that famous athlete, movie star, singer or Nobel Prize winning scientist but did not have the talent, family support or the drive to fulfill that dream, so they kept the dream alive in their child.

"The purpose of parenting is to protect and prepare our children to survive and thrive in the kind of society in which they live." (Popkin 11) It is not our job to give our child our dreams and ambitions. That is something you and your spouse need to accept. Your child is an individual with his or her own desires and expectations. You cannot force your child to be something they are not without inflicting serious psychological harm on your child. Perhaps your child will develop a passion for your passion and you can enjoy their success together. But there is a greater likelihood your child will develop interests and dreams completely unrelated to yours. Support them in either occurrence and make their dreams your dreams.

The Effects Of Your Partner's Expectations

Determine what effects, if any, your partner's expectations have on your child. You and your partner should observe your child in an environment where they feel free to express themselves. See what activities your child gravitates toward. You also want to observe how your child treats other children. Some questions to ask yourself while you are observing your child are:

1. Do you hear yourself in your child's words?
2. Is your child timid to try new things?
. Is your child aggressive with the other children?
4. Is your child controlling the play with others?
5. Is your child afraid of making mistakes?
6. Is your child acting different than the other children?

By observing your child you will be able to determine their emotional state. Is he confident and feeling good about himself or is he more aggressive and controlling? After observing your child, you and your partner can discuss how you both are influencing your child's behavior. If you see things that you do not like, ask yourself if you are putting undue pressure on your child, are you appreciating your child for who they are?

It is important to enjoy your child for who they are now and not who you hope they become. Your child's life and the relationship you experience with them now are precious. Learn to be in the moment and worry about tomorrow, tomorrow. Some suggestions for creating a happy and healthy family environment are:

- Create Family Traditions
- Play Games With Your Family
- Show Affection
- Have Fun And Laugh
- Show Interest In Each Other's Interests And Activities

You and your family are a team. Find ways to support and encourage your family members. Once you gain the support of your family, your confidence will increase. As your confidence increases your ability to accomplish your goals will increase.

Your Child Is Special But Not In The Way You Ever Expected

You understand and accept your child's learning disability, peer socialization problem or other disability. How do you learn to appreciate and enjoy your child?

You must first mourn the loss of the "ideal" child. You and your partner can talk about the child you dreamt about. The one that was popular, earned good grades, was athletic and was an all around great kid. This is your fantasy child; the one you thought about when you and your partner were pregnant. Once you and your partner start the healing process by grieving the loss of your "ideal" child, you will begin to love and appreciate your "real" child, the child that depends on you for support, guidance, nurturing, safety and comfort. This is the child that looks up to you and knows that you will always be there for them no matter the circumstance. This is the child that knows you will always love and accept who they are and not who you thought they would be. This is the child that needs you and loves you unconditionally. After all, isn't that what parenting is about, accepting your child for who they are, watching them grow and learn, living out their dreams and not yours.

Find Support Or Counseling

If you, or your partner, continue to struggle with accepting your "real" child, seek out local support groups or enter into counseling. "In general, when parents feel comfortable turning for social support when needed, adolescents are also at ease to turn to friends for information and support. Parents probably both facilitate and serve as models for adolescents' broader interaction with peers and extra familial others." (Shulman and Klein, 1982) Stay in close contact with your child's teachers. "Better coordination among teachers and between teachers and parents also is needed to facilitate and support learning, and troubleshoot problems that occur." (Wenz Gross and Siperstein) It is difficult having a child that is not like the "norm" but with support from you and your partner, your community, family and friends, you both can enjoy and love the child you have no matter their disabilities. "Families who judge favorably the assistance they receive from support group members seem to engage in a variety of positive parenting behaviors." (Bradley et al. 59)

Notes:_____

_____

_____

_____

_____

_____

_____

_____

_____

15 - Children Without Parents But No One Has Died

The best inheritance a parent can give to his children
is a few minutes of their time each day.

M. Grundler

I am sure you know couples that continue to have the same life they enjoyed without children, going out night after night, partying and caring on as if they never had children. When you ask these parents how they are able to keep the same lifestyle they enjoyed without children, you might hear them say, "Just because I have children does not mean I have to stop my life." There is some truth to this statement. Your life does not stop because you have children and you and your spouse need time to enjoy each other. (See: Your Relationship Ahead Of Your Child in Chapter 2) But to expect your life to continue unaffected is ridiculous and taken to extremes is neglectful parenting. Being parents requires you and your partner to attend to your child's needs beyond food, clothing and shelter. Your child's mental, emotional and psychological needs are neglected when you allow babysitters or any other caregivers, such as daycare centers or after school programs to primarily parent your child. Parents who fall into this category of extreme passivity toward their children should find exceptional babysitters and daycare facilities that will attend to their children's needs. (See: Looking Into Daycare in Stay At Home Parenting vs. Financial Concerns in Chapter 4) If you and your partner place a higher priority on your freedom than your children, then nothing I say here will make a difference in your passive parenting styles.

The Absent Parent

You are not a single parent, yet you have a spouse that is uninvolved with you and your children. Your spouse may have adopted the old school method of parenting where they perceive their role as the breadwinner. Once the job is over, they expect dinner on the table. After dinner, they nap or watch television before retiring to bed, only to go back to work the next day and repeat the same routine day after day completely uninvolved in your child's life. Or perhaps you have a partner who values their freedom ahead of their parental responsibilities. Meanwhile, you have been home all day with the children and would like your spouse to take over some responsibilities so you can have a moment to yourself. Whether you are coping with a parent who is physically present, but emotionally withdrawn or a parent who values their freedom before their child, the approach to resolution is the same.

Communication again is the important factor. Your spouse cannot read your mind. If you are feeling exhausted and overwhelmed due to a lack of support, you need to express yourself. Sometimes we assume that our spouse should just know how we feel, but they do not. You owe it to you, your spouse and your marriage to be upfront with each other. Use "I Messages" to tell your spouse what you would like to change and what you would like from them in the future. Then make sure you give your spouse a chance to express their feelings about your feelings and expectations. You may not get exactly what you want, but maybe you can compromise into something acceptable for both of you. By using appropriate communication, you and your spouse will understand each other and hopefully, both your needs will be met.

If your needs are not met, evaluate goals and the goals of your partner to see if your desires are even realistic. It might be something that has to change from within you. You are responsible for your own happiness. If you are not happy then it is up to you to search for that happiness. Many of my clients enter into therapy seeking help with their couple relationship. However, many times the problem exists within the individual and not the couple. It is important to remember that the individual existed before the couple and the couple existed before the child. Which means, if the individual is not happy, the couple will not be happy which concludes that the child will not be happy. Therefore, it is important that you do not lose your individuality just because you became a couple and a parent. You need to continually work on yourself in order for the family unit to be successful.

Parent Together Or Seek Counseling

Your children will benefit by having two parents in their lives. You owe it to yourself, your spouse and your children to resolve issues that are preventing you from being the best person, spouse and parent you can be. If your spouse is not meeting your expectations, the best way to resolve the issue is to speak with your spouse. Maybe your spouse is not aware of their lack of involvement. The more you and your spouse communicate appropriately, the happier you, your partner and your family will become. If the task of attaining equal parenting responsibility is proving too difficult, consider seeking professional help in the form of a counselor or psychologist to help both of you understand why you, or your spouse, have these feelings of disinterest. You deserve to be happy. Marriage and parenting should not feel like a life sentence.

Your Husband Is A Bad Father

Many women in my private practice sessions have expressed negative feelings about their husbands not living up to their expectations as fathers. Many of these women express a similar fantasy. Their husbands would awaken to the sound of the baby crying, rise out of bed and bring the baby to them in bed for the baby feeding. Another common fantasy expressed in sessions was that the husband would be equally involved in all aspects of their child's life. The dad would come home from work and immediately run to the baby and play with the baby, allowing the mom to take a bubble bath or relax for a few minutes. The fantasy continues with the dad helping with baths, changing diapers, feeding the baby, etc. When the baby gets sick, the mom fantasizes that the dad will help with the late night baths and medications and when the baby cries, the dad will take over and help calm the baby down. Does this sound like a familiar fantasy? You moms, or future moms, may have other twists of your own but my advice to every mother in my private practice is the same as the advice I am providing in this book;

your fantasy is just that, a fantasy, and you need to accept the reality of your situation. You may have a husband who is a wonderful dad, but he probably will never live up to the expectations you created in your mind. You had all these perfect ideas of how your husband would be as a dad, but know that the dream will never come true. So maybe he doesn't run home from a long day at work and take care of the children. Or maybe he doesn't help with late night feedings. Or maybe you can count on one hand how many times he fed, changed, clothed and bathed the baby. These were all your perfect dad fantasies. They were never his fantasy. He might be a great dad, but instead of doing things your way, he interacts with his child his way.

You might have to learn to let things go and learn to enjoy who he is as a person and a dad. If you have honestly tried to accept your child's dad, but the frustration does not subside, communicate those frustrations to him. After communicating your feeling of frustration, you must then listen to his feelings about being a dad and how he feels about your frustrations as well.

Sometimes, when expressing frustrations, you might feel compelled to focus on the negative and not see the positive. So when you and your husband talk about your fantasies make sure you take a good look at what your husband is doing well. A good rule to implement when expressing frustrations is to express two positives for every negative. This will force you to see the positive aspects of your partner and shows your partner you recognize and appreciate your partner's efforts. Imagine how you would feel if you had to listen to your husband read off a laundry list of what he believed were your negative characteristics. It would certainly be easier to hear the negative characteristics after hearing some positives.

Your Expectations Are Too High

If you are struggling to find two positives to describe your husband as a dad, perhaps you and your partner need to try this exercise. On a piece of paper list ten qualities, characteristics or attributes your husband can do to classify him as a good dad: your perfect dad wish list. Have your husband do the same; only his list will be titled, 'Ten qualities, characteristics or attributes that would classify me as a good dad". Compare the two lists to see if what you believe makes a good dad is what your husband believes constitutes a good dad. If your goals are very different, this will give you the opportunity to discuss why they are important to you. The point of the exercise is to allow both sides to express their opinions in a clear, concise and constructive manner. Utilizing a pen and paper rather than the spoken word lessens the potential for escalating emotions, resulting in a heated argument or complete breakdown in communication. Reading the two lists will allow you and your husband to see if you have similar opinions about the qualities of a good dad. Keep in mind that your husband will probably not agree, nor will he adhere to every item on your list. You and your husband may learn characteristics of being a good dad that you had not considered before trying this exercise. Once you compare your lists and are in agreement with some or all of the ten points, you and your husband can discuss ways that he can implement these points into his parenting. The objective is to present your concerns to your husband in an open, non confrontational approach. Do not gloss over the positive parenting points you both agree constitutes a good dad. Express your appreciation for the wonderful qualities you both agree he possesses. When discussing the points of contention, avoid a heated debate at all costs. Remember that your goal is to express your concerns in such a way as to encourage your husband to change into the dad you desire and your child deserves. With this goal in mind, if your husband feels he is being attacked, you will achieve a less desirable result. This exercise allows you to acknowledge the reality of your situation and communicate with your spouse your realistic expectations. This exercise will allow you to accept your partner for the father he is and not the dad you thought he would be.

Brad Says, "Children Are A Distraction!"

Children demand attention. They make you slow down and teach them about the world, but only if you let them. And if you ignore them, you are teaching them that you are not interested in what they think, do, or say. So being a "Dad" means you will have to reassess your priorities. "Dad"s need to be selective about the amount of sports they watch. "Dad"s need to find the time to spend good quality time with their kids. It should be difficult to follow your favorite sports and impossible to follow the sports you like only a little. "Dad"s will give up the rapid climb to success in the business world for a slower methodical climb. Being a "Dad" is hard work. Being a "Father" is not. (See: Brad Explains The Difference Between Being a "Dad" vs. Being a "Father" in Chapter 2)

A Tip From A Dad About How To Prioritize Your Child vs. Sports

You are a "Father" who wants to be a "Dad" but you do not know how. Here is some practical, no nonsense advise on how to prioritizing your sporting events. If you have a choice between watching a regular season game in one sport and a playoff game in another sport, then I recommend you do not watch the regular season game and use that time to spend with the kids. Regular season games in the beginning of the season are less important than regular season games at the end of the season. If it is difficult to miss even one early regular season game, then at least give up the beginning of the games. Only watch the second half of football or basketball games or sixth inning to the end of baseball games. If you are unable to give up even one second of any sporting events on the weekends, then you need to force yourself to have the energy to spend time with the kids on the weekdays. Just one hour a day after work will help swing the pendulum from being a "Father" to being a "Dad". I think you get the idea. Prioritize and make time for your kids or else I say, "Congratulations, you are a successful "Father"! (See: Brad Explains The Difference Between Being a "Dad" vs. Being a "Father" in Chapter 2)

A Tip From A Dad About How To Prioritize Your Child vs. Your Career

A 1991 Gallup poll found that a majority of American men 59 percent derive "a greater sense of satisfaction from caring for their family than from a job well done at work. [Most men today] no longer define being a good father almost exclusively in terms of the ability to provide economically." (Levine and Pittinsky 14) Here is some practical, no nonsense advise to a "Father" who wants to become a "Dad" from a time management and priorities management perspective. If you are an average forty hour a work week Dad with no other means of income to support the family, or if you are a divorced or widowed Dad, then obviously this is a lot tougher than a Dad who can work from home or who has a wife who works. But here are some things you can do to improve your ability to be a Dad. Keep track of the number of hours you are talking, doing homework, playing or just spending good quality time with your kids. If you subtract the 40 hours a week you spend at work from a   day, 24 hour a day week, you are left with 168 hours in a week, which yields 128 hours. Now subtract sleep, assuming 8 hours a day for   days: 128 56= 2 hours.   2 hours divided by 24 hours in a day, leaves you with a grand total of   days to find quality time to spend with your children. The great thing about kids is they love any amount of time you spend with them and you can use sports or your career as your reward for spending time with your children. If you can spend at least one hour a night with your children during the week after work, then finding time to watch sports on the weekend or having to go on long business trips or work extra hours on the weekend will be much easier and guilt free. If you feel too exhausted to spend time with the kids on the weekdays after work or your career is too important to not work long hours Monday to Friday, then I suggest setting aside a Saturday or Sunday morning to devote purely to the kids. If you cannot even do this for your children, then congratulations, you are a successful "Father"! (See: Brad Explains The Difference Between Being a "Dad" vs. Being a "Father" in Chapter 2)

Your Wife Is A Bad Mother

You met and married a woman you thought would be the perfect wife without thinking about your expectations of her as a mother. Men typically don't think about children or how their wife will perform as a mother. Men just assume all women are naturally terrific mothers because they are women. Generally speaking, the great majority of the time you would be safe to assume they can do a better than adequate job of raising your children. Before having children, you learned to live with each other's good and bad habits through good times and bad. Overall she was everything you could ever want in a wife and so you expected, when children came into the picture, she would continue to be this wonderful woman you married with the ability to have dinner ready for you when you came home from a long day at work. Why would anything change after having children? You expected the house to be cleaned, laundry done and put away before you had children, so why should anything change after you have children? Everything should remain the same with just a few extra chores around the house, resulting from the added mouths to feed, baths and getting the children ready for bed. With children in the house, you imagined the smell of fresh baked cookies and your wife looking beautiful as she greets you at the door. Dinner would be on the table, the children are behaving like perfect little gentlemen and ladies and the house is clean from your wife's tireless efforts to be the perfect wife and mother. That was your fantasy before children.

The reality is something entirely different. You come home from a long day at work to find the house smelling like dirty diapers. Your dinner is in the freezer waiting to be prepared by you. The children are dirty and smelly waiting for you to give them a bath. The laundry basket is overflowing with dirty clothes and the house is filled with toys and dirty dishes. You ask yourself, "Where did everything go wrong?"

Unfortunately, if you are like most American households today, both parents must work to survive. The "Ozzie and Harriett" or even the "Brady Bunch" days are a dream of the past. "Whether in single or dual parent families, one of the common denominators among working fathers is feeling torn by two emotions: guilt for not spending more time with their children and worry about being able to make a living. " (Levine and Pittinsky 21) With both parents in the work force, the parent who arrives home first prepares dinner for the family. Children will generally fend for themselves if they are old enough to make dinner and the house is rarely clean. Some of you are saying that your wife is a full time mom and she still does not have dinner ready or a clean house. Obviously you certainly would have a stronger case for a clean house and food on the table when you arrive home, but in either situation the remedy remains the same.

Express Your Feelings

Remember not to ridicule or belittle her but express your feelings in a calm and respectful manner. You and your wife can do the same exercise that was mentioned in the previous section. On a piece of paper, list ten qualities, characteristics or attributes your wife can do to classify her as a good wife and mom: your perfect wife and mom wish list. Have your wife do the same; only her list will be titled, 'Ten qualities, characteristics or attributes that would classify her as a good wife and mom". Compare the two lists to see if what you believe constitutes a good mom is what your wife believes constitute a good mom. If your goals are very different, this will give you the opportunity to discuss why they are important to you. The point of the exercise is to allow both sides to express their opinions in a clear, concise and constructive manner. Utilizing a pen and paper rather than the spoken word lessens the potential for escalating emotions to result in a heated argument or complete breakdown in communication. Reading the two lists will allow you and your wife to see if you have similar opinions of what you believe are the qualities of a good mom. Keep in mind that your wife will probably not agree, nor will she adhere to every item on your list. You and your wife may learn characteristics of being a good mom that you had not considered before trying this exercise. Once you compare your lists and are in agreement with some or all of the ten points, you and your wife can discuss ways that she can implement these points into her parenting. The objective is to present your concerns to your wife in an open, non confrontational approach. Do not gloss over the points you both agree constitute a good mom that she is already doing well. Express your appreciation for the wonderful qualities you both agree she possesses. When discussing the points of possible contention, avoid a heated debate at all costs. Remember that your goal is to express your concerns in such a way as to encourage your wife to change into the mom you desire and your children deserve. With this goal in mind, if your wife feels she is being attacked, you will achieve a less desirable result.

Your Wife Is Not Your Mother

If a great mom raised you, your wife might never live up to your expectations of her as a mother. The key to having a successful relationship is to accept each other as you are. If you continue to struggle with your wife not meeting your expectations, try to work on a compromise, maybe she can meet you half way. You might also have to drop some of your expectations and learn to enjoy the mother she is capable of being.

Notes:_____

_____

_____

_____

_____

_____

_____

_____

16 - Coping With A Sick Parent

Character cannot be developed in ease and quiet.
Only through experience of trial and suffering can the soul
be strengthened, ambition inspired, and success achieved.

Helen Keller

I have a husband who is a great dad. He will go the extra mile for our children. He is attentive and really seems to enjoy spending time with our children. He seems to be able to play with them non stop until he becomes ill! His colds and fevers can put him out of commission for what seems like weeks! I'm sure you heard the expression that if men could have babies there would be no children. Well, that is definitely true with my husband. All kidding aside, when a parent is sick, whether it is with the flu, a cold or something serious, it becomes very strenuous for the healthy parent. The entire burden falls on the healthy parent's shoulders. Now your role has changed. Not only do you have to take care of your children, the house, a pet and possibly your job, you also have the added responsibility of caring for a sick partner.

Caring For Everyone And Everything
Without Losing Your Sanity

By caring for yourself first! I know what you're thinking, "How can I take care of me when I have a thousand other things to take care of?" You just do it. Taking care of a sick loved one can be very stressful. If you do not take some time for yourself, you could become sick and that would not benefit anyone. When you set aside some time during the day for yourself, you will be more energized and physically and mentally ready to care of your family. How many minutes should you set aside? That depends on your needs. Ask yourself, "What amount of time per day will give me the energy necessary to care for everyone and everything without losing my sanity?" If you are the type of person who cannot determine an amount of time that is appropriate for you, then I will tell you to take 15 minutes per day. If you need more than 15 minutes, then take more than 15 minutes. Your house might not be as tidy as it would be normally and your laundry might be piled a little high, but at least you will have some free time to take a moment for yourself. You might miss some of your children's sporting events or make peanut butter and jelly for dinner. As long is this is not normal behavior, your children will survive. Fortunately I never heard of a child starving on peanut butter and jelly sandwiches! If you appear relaxed and in control, your children will adjust to your momentary lapse of normal behavior. I also advise you to ask for help. Call a friend or a family member to watch the kids or pick something up at the grocery store. The good news is that colds or flues do not last forever. Know that in a few days, or perhaps a week, your partner will be feeling better and will be back to their old self.

Coping With A Long Term
Or Permanent Illness

When the sickness is more severe or one parent has suffered a debilitating injury, the frustration for the healthy parent can prove to be overwhelming. The rules for coping remain the same. Take care of yourself and do not be afraid to ask for help. The problem is that unfortunately it will take longer than a week and your resolve, patience and persistence will be severely tested, making the rules for coping all the more important to keep your sanity and your health.

Dealing with a severe illness or a recent disability is very traumatic. Not only has your roles changed, you are now the provider and the caretaker for the entire family. That can be overwhelming and very demanding. You will go through phases of grief, denial, depression, anger, bargaining and finally acceptance. Give yourself time to grieve. It is a tremendous loss. You lost your healthy spouse. The one you relied on to be an equal part of your team. Allow your children to grieve as well. They also lost the healthy parent they counted on to always be there. The parent who is going through this life change will also need time to grieve. Everyone grieves differently. This is a time where the family should be honest with each other and communicates their feelings of loss, sadness, anger, fear, etc.

Your family will grow stronger from this situation if you all communicate and listen to one another. Remember that you are not alone. You all have each other. Your family illness can actually be a time where you learn to appreciate each other and reconnect on a different level.

Find A Support Group

Finding a support group in your community or on the internet is a terrific way to share your experiences with others who may be experiencing similar frustrations.

Notes:_____

_____

_____

_____

_____

_____

_____

_____

_____

17 - The Death Of A Parent

What we have done for ourselves alone dies with us;
what we have done for others and the world remains
and is immortal.

Albert Pike

Raising your children after the death of your spouse is quite challenging and emotional. You are dealing with your own grief at the same time you need to be a parent to your children who are also grieving. "Specifically, attention needs to be paid to those variables that mediate the parental death child distress relation, and are modifiable. " (Thompson et al. 5) After the death of a parent, children want reassurance from the living parent that everything will be all right. It is difficult to accomplish this goal when you are unsure of the answers.

Your Children Should Be Crying With You

People say, "Once you and your children have closure you will be able to let go and move on." Nothing could be further from truth. There is no closure for the loss of a loved one. You will heal and be happy again but you will forever be changed. Your children will never have their biological parent back and you will never have your partner back. You and your children will have feelings of anger, guilt, sadness, and many more. "It also may result in acting out behavior by the child or guilt related to the child's beliefs about possible personal culpability in causing or being unable to prevent the death. Without open communication, such misconceptions cannot be rectified." (Raveis, Siegel and Karus 165) The best way to heal from this traumatic loss is to talk about the deceased parent. Show pictures, talk about good times and talk about things you miss. You might believe that you must be strong for the children, but it is okay for your children to see you cry. Do not interpret strength as never letting your children see you cry. If your children do not see or, at least know, you are sad and have cried over the loss of your partner and their parent, your children may interpret your "strength", or not crying, as a sign that it is not acceptable to cry. Your crying gives them permission to cry as well.

Do Not Change The Rules

Your children will begin to find comfort in things returning back to normal. I know you are thinking that nothing can be normal again but that is not true. You can apply the same structure and rules in your home that you did with your spouse. Your children will feel safe when the same limits and boundaries are implemented. They will often find comfort when you can go back to your same routine.

Find A Support Network For You

A support network will also help with the healing process. You will need time for yourself to grieve and to rejuvenate yourself. Allow that time for yourself. You are not a superhero! If you do not take care of yourself, you will not be emotionally available for your children. As you require a break from the situation so does your child. To have fun again does not mean you forgot the deceased parent. Your child will forever be changed but it does not mean they cannot enjoy life again. It just means that life will be different for them and for you. It is healthy for your children to go out and do kid things. It will give them a chance to get away emotionally and see that even though they miss their parent, they can still have fun again.

There are also many resources in your community to help you during this time. You can call your local church, schools or community center for counseling and support groups.

Find A Good Therapist For Your Child

Depending upon the age of your child and the circumstances surrounding the death of your partner, your child will experience varying degrees of grief. "Results are strongly suggestive that mode of death predicts variations in a youth's post death symptomatology. " (Thompson et al. 5) Seeking the services of a mental health professional is recommended. When your child suffers a broken bone, you would certainly take your child to the doctor to heal the broken bone. Your child's heart is broken. Take your child's broken heart to a mental health professional so they can help your child heal their pain. If you also feel the need to speak to a mental health professional, please do so.

Some Good News For Your Child's Future

To end this chapter on a positive note there are some unique advantages for children who suffer the loss of a parent. Death is generally unintentional, post divorce conflict is not a factor and widowed mothers can receive more economic support in the form of survivors insurance. "So, although children who experience the death of a father may be greatly affected emotionally, the long term consequences in terms of their family formation and achievement may be smaller for these other reasons." (McLanahan and Teitler 89)

Notes:_____

_____

_____

_____

_____

_____

_____

_____

18 - Grandparents Raising Grandchildren

The whole business of marshaling one's energies becomes more and more important as one grows older.

Hume Cronyn

You raised your children and you thought your job was done. But instead of enjoying your retirement, you find yourself thrown back into the role of raising young children. The only difference is that you are 20 years older and they are your grandchildren. You either entered into this new family due to the death of your children or your children were unable to raise their own. Now you are attending back to school functions, establishing bedtime routines and caring for sick children. How do you learn to enjoy being a parent again?

If you are like most grandparents you accepted this responsibility without hesitation. But the strain of raising your grandchildren can be overwhelming. Along with the challenges of feeling anger and resentment towards your own children are the challenges your grandchildren face over losing a parent.

You must first grieve the loss of your child. Whether it was due to a death or court ordered loss of parental rights, your child was not able to raise his or her own children. That can be very depressing and traumatic for you and your grandchild. Your grandchildren are left feeling betrayed, abandoned and alone. There will be a lot of adjustments for you, your partner and your grandchildren. You and your new family need time to become accustomed to family members redefining their role. Your grandchildren now take on the role of your children and you take on the role of their parents. You are now responsible for these children.

I advise you and your partner to get support. There are support groups for grandparents raising grandchildren. You can go to your local church, community center or schools in your area to learn when these groups meet. The importance of the groups is to let you know that you are not alone. Some organizations and websites for grandparents are:

The Foundation for Grandparenting,

www.grandparenting.org

Grandparent InformationCenter, AARP, www.aarp.org,

800 424 410

Grandparents As Parents, 562 924 996

National Coalition of Grandparents, Madison, Wisc., 608

2 8 8 51

Your Limitations

Another important consideration is for you and your partner to know your limits. Unfortunately age plays a role in what our bodies can and cannot do. Assuming the unavailability of other relatives to care for your grandchildren in the event of your death, who would be able to take the children? You are the only stable family member left in your grandchildren's lives. It is imperative you take care of yourself. The added stress of taking care of young children for both you and your partner can have a negative impact on your health. It is absolutely essential you maintain your health to ensure your grandchildren do not become wards of the state to be raised by strangers in the event of your death. Set time aside for you and your partner to take care of yourself. If you are widowed then taking care of yourself is your absolute highest priority. Make sure you get your medical check ups and eat properly. Increase your support network so others can help care for your grandchildren for a few hours or a day every week while you care for your mental, physical and emotional needs. It is also important for you to take care of your relationship with your partner. Neglecting the relationship will only add to the stress of your household. Your grandchildren depend on you. You are all they have. So you owe it to them to take care of yourself as well as your relationship. (See: Your Relationship Ahead Of Your Child in Chapter 2)

Give Your Grandchild Permission To Grieve

It might sound ridiculous to give your grandchild permission to express their feelings. This is important because your grandchild might feel they are betraying you if they show signs they miss their parents. Assure your grandchild that you are not going anywhere. Your grandchild does not want to lose you and does not want to betray you. That is why it is important to talk to them about their feelings and give them some feeling words such as: "I'm sad, angry, afraid, etc". By doing this, you are providing them with comfort and safety to talk about the loss of their parents.

Your Role Has Changed

Many grandparents enjoy buying toys and candy for their grandchildren. They shower their grandchildren with attention and enjoy leaving the unenviable task of parenting to their grandchildren's parents. As a grandparent raising your grandchildren, your role has changed. You are now faced with taking over the disciplinary responsibility, going to school functions and being involved in their day to day lives like you did when you raised your own children. So, how do you take over this role?

Your instinct might be to let your grandchildren do what they would not have been able to do when their parents were around. You may feel they have been through so much you do not want to add to their misery. Perhaps you feel uncomfortable disciplining your grandchild as you never disciplined them when they were not in your care. You are in the unenviable position of having to set limits with your own grandchildren and applying consequences when they break the rules. Setting clear boundaries for your grandchildren is important because your grandchildren's world has just been turned upside down. Limits will enable them to feel safe and secure again. It is also important for you to try to get into a routine. Again this will provide your grandchildren with a sense of safety and comfort. Now that you are essentially parents again, many of the topics in "Good Parents Bad Parenting" apply to you.

If you have custody due to neglect or abuse you will be facing other challenges. It might be the first time where your grandchild is experiencing structure, discipline and consistency. You might see your grandchild rebelling and pushing you to your limits. Consider seeking outside support such as a therapist or a school counselor to assist you with this adjustment. Your grandchild will likely experience abandonment issues that can cause behavioral problems. Again counseling might be the best option.

Notes:_____

_____

_____

_____

_____

_____

_____

_____

_____

19 - School Bells Are Ringing And Your Child Is Singing The Blues

Education is what survives when what has been learned has been forgotten.

B. F. Skinner

One of your child's biggest stressors is school. In my private practice, when summer vacation arrives, every child expresses feelings of relief as if a great weight has been lifted from their shoulders. At the beginning of the school year, the pressure to get good grades returns, a nightly struggle to complete all their homework, new teachers, new friends, transition from elementary to middle and middle to high schools are expressed to me in sessions.

Alleviating The Stress

You and your parenting partner set goals for your child, but like our society, you probably established results oriented goals, which is a natural way to approach goal setting. The goals may be for your child to maintain an A or B average. If your child is generally receiving a B+ average, but is struggling with one subject, then your goals may be to maintain the B+ average, but to work harder on one subject to bring the low grade up. However, these are your goals and may not be your child's goals. You might expect your child to achieve nothing less than a B on his report card but your child might only be capable of C level work. Instead of mandating your goal expectations to your child, include your child in the goal setting process. At the beginning of the school year, discuss with your child the academic achievements they would like to set for themselves. Once they set these goals, with your assistance, have your child share with you the means by which he, or she, will obtain these goals. Here is an example:

Child's goals:

    Do all my homework on a daily basis

    Study for test   0 min. a day

    Review homework with parents on a daily basis

Ways of Achieving Goals:

Do homework from 4:00 4: 0

Finish any homework from 4:45 5:15

Study for test from 5: 0 6:00

Review homework with parents at   :00

This is a very structured goal setting example, clearly laying out exactly what you and your child expect on a daily basis to achieve their goals. Instead of determining a grade result and expecting your child to determine their own level of effort on a daily basis to achieve your goals, grades are not mentioned within this goal setting structure. The result of your child's clear expectation of necessary work on a daily basis should result in good grades. If your child chooses to go away from his goals, then a consequence will typically result in poor grades.

You and your partner's goals should be to stay involved with your child's school progress, monitoring his or her daily commitment to studying and homework and contacting your child's teacher regularly through email, phone or a website your child's teacher may have established to keep parents aware of their child's progress and a calendar of assignments due. With this method of tracking your child's progress, consequences for not following the scheduled daily requirements to maintain good grades should be implemented as the deviation from the agreed upon schedule occurs, not when the grades arrive at the end of the year. If you and your partner adequately monitored your child's progress throughout the year and the poor grades continue, then the poor grade should be a shared disappointment for you, your partner and your child.

Signs Of Problems Can Start In School

When a child is feeling anxiety or depressed, declining school performance can be the first sign something is wrong. You might notice a decrease in grades along with a decrease in your child's motivation. Other signs something is wrong is when your child makes excuses to stay home from school or if you notice a drop in peer interaction. Monitoring your child's school performance and speaking often with your child's teacher increase the likelihood you will address the situation with your child before it gets out of hand. Parents might be afraid to see the signs because they will have to admit something is wrong with their child.

I know, as a parent, I don't like the feelings associated with a potential problem in my own child. My husband and I communicate often about how we perceive our own children to check if we view our child's mental and physical abilities, potential anxieties or apprehensions to be sure we are not in denial about our own children as is so easy to do. We act as a safety valve for each other to be sure we are not ignoring a potential problem that may need to be addressed. Many times our fears about our children's anxiety or development are just phases or normal child behavior that will eventually correct itself. Sometimes our concerns need to be addressed and we take proactive steps to correct the problem as soon as possible to minimize long term ramifications. We would rather address the signs now instead of wishing that we did something when it is too late. By continuously speaking with your partner about your children, you will only have to correct an occasional molehill instead of a mountain of a problem in the future.

Let's Play School

If your child is having a difficult time expressing their feelings about school, here is an effective game you can play to improve the communication. This game will help connect your child's feelings to his or her actions and in the process you will learn more about your child.

You will need:

Poster Board

1 die

Game pieces or coins

Marker

On poster board draw a picture of a schoolhouse. Inside the house draw square spaces. Make the squares large enough to write in. Do not forget to draw a start square. You do not need to draw an end square because there are only winners, no losers, in this game. Within the squares write questions that you would like to know. The following are suggestions. Feel free to add any that you feel would benefit your child.

What do you like about school?

When are you happiest at school?

What makes you mad about school?

Who are your friends?

Who do you eat lunch with?

Who do you play with at recess?

What subjects are hard for you?

What subjects are easy for you?

Did anyone ever bully you at school?

You could also add squares that say:

Hit a kid. What could you have done instead?

Yelled at teacher. What could you have done instead?

Not listening in class. Miss a turn

Didn't turn in homework. What could you do to remember to turn in your homework?

New kid in school. What can you do to be their friend?

If your child has trouble making friends, ask questions about how to make friends. Use the squares to implement ideas that concern you. This game format will enable your family to build a relationship on appropriate ways to communicate and interact. In this type of environment your child will feel safe to express their feelings to you and your partner.

To Play:

Roll the die and move accordingly. Answer questions on the square. Again there are no winners or losers. Game is over when you and your spouse feel that your concerns have been addressed and your child feels more comfortable expressing his or her feelings to you.

Notes:_____

_____

_____

_____

_____

_____

_____

_____

_____

20 - Your Child, Sex, Drugs and Alcohol

Adolescence is a period of rapid changes.
Between the ages of 12 and 17, for example,
a parent ages as much as 20 years.

Anonymous

I hear many parents ask, "What age should we talk to our children about sex, drugs and alcohol?" I always answer that question; "You should talk to your children about sex, drugs and alcohol from the time they are toddlers." You may be wondering how to talk to a toddler about complex subjects as sex, drugs and alcohol. I certainly do not advocate parents renting triple XXX videos and allowing their children to experiment with narcotics or alcohol of any kind.

Age Appropriate Sex

Talk to your toddler in age appropriate language. Toddlers are not too young to educate about the differences between the sexes. As your child ages they will ask more questions as their curiosity about sex grows. Always answer their questions in age appropriate answers. A toddler should be taught body parts, using the adult body part names, not the cute kid names often used. Many teenagers, and even adults, are embarrassed by the words vagina or penis. The reason for the embarrassment stems from a child's interpreting your use of the cute kid name in place of the perfectly acceptable adult body part name as words that should not be spoken aloud. Children are taught from a very young age that speaking or hearing the adult body part name is shameful. If you and your partner teach your children the correct terminology to both the male and female body parts, they will not be ashamed or embarrassed when they hear these words used as a teenager or adult. When your child begins to recognize the difference between you and your spouse or between themselves and a sibling, this is the perfect opportunity to teach toddlers the difference between girls and boys. Congratulations, you just had your first age appropriate sex talk.

When your child is approximately   years old, you might see them explore their body. This is a very delicate stage.

You do not want to humiliate them or shame them into believing something is wrong with their body or that there is something wrong with what they are doing to their body. You want to inform them that they need to do that in private, i.e. the bathroom or their bedroom. You want them to be proud of their body and not make your child think they are doing something wrong.

Address your child's questions no matter how embarrassing. My four year old started asking me about body parts while we were in a crowded ladies room. For anyone who has a four year old, you know that four year olds do not have volume control. The quieter I answered his questions the louder he asked them. Let your child know that their questions are good questions and that you will talk to them when you can talk privately. Make sure that you definitely address the questions when you get to a place where you are alone.

Masturbation Is A Sin

"The sexual behavior of those men and women who had masturbated during preadolescence and/or early adolescence was no different than the sexual behavior of those who had not masturbated in either preadolescence or early adolescence." (Leitenberg, Detzer and Srebnik) You may have been taught to believe masturbation is a sin. Some parents have told their children that they will go blind if they masturbate. Some religious beliefs also condemn masturbation as a sin. I certainly do not advocate telling children that touching their own body is wrong. Touching our bodies is how we experiment, learn and feel good about ourselves. You want to let your child know there is an appropriate time and place to touch and explore. This is also a good time to talk about good touching and bad touching. They need to know they have control over who can and cannot touch them. When a touch doesn't feel good, such as an unwanted hug or a kiss, they should say, "No, I don't like that. Please stop." As parents you want to reinforce their boundaries by respecting their wishes when they do not wish to hug and kiss you as well. This can be difficult when you want to show your love for your child and your child is asking you not to hug. Fortunately most children will eventually hug and kiss you when they know it is a choice and not a requirement.

Talking About Sex

From clients and others in my daily life, I have heard the argument that talking about sex gives permission to your child to participate in sexual activity. Nothing could be further from the truth. Clearly expressing your beliefs about sex, how you expect your children to feel, act and react to potential sexual encounters and conveying to your children that they can talk to you about their feelings about sex will generally delay sexual encounters and will foster healthy attitudes about the opposite sex, premarital sex and committed relationships. Educating your child about sex is not condoning sexual experimentation. You are informing your child of all available options and the consequences of those options. Going back to the explanation about using adult terminology for body parts, the same is true when you do not discuss sex with your older child or teenager. By not talking about sex, you are conveying to your child that there is something shameful, or secretive, in both talking and participating in sex. You want your child to come to you with questions and concerns they might have about sex rather than receiving advice from others that do not have your child's best interest at heart. If your goal is to prevent your child from experimenting with sex until a certain age or until they are married, then tell them what you wish for them to do and explain your reasons for your beliefs. The uncomfortable feeling you may experience when talking about sex to your child typically stems from your parents inability to communicate with you about sex. If the feeling is so overwhelming that you struggle to discuss this topic with your child, go to the local library and find age appropriate books that you and your child can read together. Keep in mind that informing your child about sex can prevent sexually transmitted diseases, unwanted pregnancies and can potentially save your child's life.

Talking About Drugs And Alcohol

You want to know what age is an appropriate age to discuss drugs and alcohol with your child. I would love to give you a definitive answer, but the answer depends on your family history and your child.

Your Family History

Look at your spouse and your family history chart and see what, if any, role drugs and alcohol play in your family history. If there is a history of addiction in your family, then your children are more likely to be addicted to drugs or alcohol themselves. Parents who are alcoholics or problem drinkers place their children at increased risk for drug dependence. Studies suggest that a tendency toward alcoholism may run in the family. According to the American Academy of Pediatrics website (http://www.aap.org/), one out of five young adults with an alcoholic parent have become addicted to drugs. If you or your spouse have an addiction or come from addictive families you are probably aware that an addictive family learns not to talk about the addiction. Obviously this is not the appropriate way to handle the situation but it is a learned way. It is up to you and your spouse to break the cycle.

No Family History: When Is The Appropriate Age?

If you do not come from a family of addiction, it is still important for you and your partner to educate your children on the effects of drugs and alcohol. Unfortunately in today's society many school age children as young as elementary school age are aware and experiment with drugs and various alcoholic beverages. The American Academy of Pediatrics website (http://www.aap.org/) states that one out of three fourth graders believe that drinking is a "big problem" in their age group. About one out of seven fourth graders already have consumed alcohol to the point of intoxication. Four out of ten sixth graders say there is pressure from other students to drink alcohol. Three million children ages fourteen to seventeen are problem drinkers. Because of these statistics, many schools have implemented the DARE Program to help educate children about the effects of drugs and alcohol. It is also our job as parents to provide education to our children on the effects of drugs and alcohol. There are many age appropriate books on this subject for you and your child to read together. Visit your local library or bookstore to find books that are appropriate for you and your child.

Talking Does Not Give Permission

Talking about drugs and alcohol arms your child with the knowledge of the effects that drugs and alcohol can have on their mind, body and spirit. If you, your partner or your children have difficulty discussing drugs, alcohol or sex, an effective technique is to address these issues in a non threatening way. An effective technique to ease the tension and allow the communication to begin is through a game. By playing a game, you, your partner and your child might feel less intimidated by the severity of the topic and might be more likely to open up. Here is an example of a game that you might want to implement. Feel free to change or add questions to fit your family's needs.

Talking About Teenage Issues Game

You will need:

1 die

Poster Board

Game pieces or coins

Markers

Your poster board will be your game board. You can make the game as simple or as creative as you wish.

Draw an outline of your game. I typically draw a mouth outline to emphasize communication. Once you draw your shape, draw squares around the outside. Make the squares big enough to write questions or comments. Make sure you include a start square. I usually do not include an end square because the line of communication never should end. In your squares you should write questions or comments that you or your child would like to know. Here is list of sample questions and comments:

Why are drugs bad?

What are your views about drugs?

You can ask any question about drugs.

What do you think about peer pressure?

Ask any question on peer pressure.

Talk about a time you were pressured by your peers.

Say something encouraging about your parent/child

Talk about teen pregnancy.

Ask any question about sex.

What are your feelings about birth control?

Talk about sexual transmitted diseases.

What are your feelings about alcohol?

Why do people drink?

Do you know anyone who drinks or does drugs? If yes, what are your views about them?

Ask any question about alcohol.

Has alcohol affected your life?

Share something about parties.

What are your fears?

Feel free to add any questions that you or even your child might want on this game. The goal of the game is to encourage your family to discuss important issues in a supportive, non threatening and loving environment. This environment will allow you and your child the openness to talk about issues that can be otherwise difficult to address.

To Play:

Roll the die and move game piece accordingly. You can make it more interesting by adding "Miss A Turn" or "Move Ahead" squares. Game is over when all issues are addressed.

Notes:_____

_____

_____

_____

_____

_____

_____

_____

_____

21 - Interfaith Relationships –
Maybe Mom Was Right

A great marriage is not when the 'perfect couple' comes together. It is when an imperfect couple learns to enjoy their differences.

Dave Meurer

As if relationships were not difficult enough, you married someone with a different religious background. Many people who marry outside their religion have a preconceived idea that their children will decide what religion they will follow and it won't be a big deal. The reality is very different for a child. A young child relies on their parents to make choices for them. "A child whose parents, school, and church all teach him 'the one way,' may seem narrow to those of another way, but he has no conflict within himself for he is certain and sure, has no decisions to make, and no pangs of conscience if he follows 'the straight and narrow path.'"

(Bossard and Boll 12) Children want and need structure in their lives; they are looking for absolute answers to learn the rules of their new world. When your child asks a question that involves religion, do you know enough about your partner's religion to answer it adequately to represent both religious beliefs? If your child decides at a young age they want to follow your partner's religion, will you discourage their early decision or will you support your child's choice to follow your partner's religion before you really had an opportunity to "sell" your religion? You may have lost your child to your partner's religion before you ever had a chance to show them the beauty of your religious beliefs. Even if you believe you could accept your child choosing your partner's religion, your child is aware of the excitement you will feel if your child chooses your religion. Since your child will want to please both of you, deciding which religion to follow is the same as asking your child to choose which parent they like more.

Counseling Before Marriage

Before you and your partner enter into matrimony, you should discuss how you intend to raise your children. "Any religion that has any value and vitality extends its beliefs into deeds observances, abstinences, good works; and the more vital the religion the more true this is. Also, the older the religion the more these expectations of conduct have hardened into strict requirements." (Bossard and Boll 5) However, most couples gloss over this issue, believing they will deal with the issue when they have children and that their love will get them through any rough spots. You might find your once flexible partner, uncompromising when your little bundle of joy arrives. As most people reading this book are already married with children, recommending marriage counseling before marriage is like saying, "I told you so", so we will move into some practical advice for coping with interfaith marriage issues.

Coping With Your Inflexible Partner

Obviously, the first step is to address the issue of religion with your spouse in an open and honest way. This is a time where you and your spouse can learn what religion means to both of you. Here is an example of an exercise you and your spouse can do together:

1. Each of you should separately define what religion means to you.
2. What role did religion play in your family of origin?
. What is the importance of religion for both of you?
4. What role does religion play in your lives today?
5. Where and how do you practice your religious beliefs?

6. What role do both of you want religion to play in the lives of your children and why?

. What is your definition of spirituality?

8. What role did/does spirituality play in your lives?

9. What role do you want spirituality to play in the lives of your children?

These are just some examples of questions you and your spouse can discuss with each other. By answering these questions, you and your spouse will recognize the religious values that you both wish to instill in your children. My husband and I disagree on the following point: I believe your religious and spiritual values are like opinions. Opinions are not facts and therefore cannot be right or wrong. My husband believes an opinion can be wrong. Therefore your religious and spiritual values can be right or wrong as well. What is your opinion on abortion? Whatever you believe you probably also believe the other side is wrong. Regardless of who you believe is correct, your religious and spiritual values are what you believe. How you incorporate your beliefs into your daily life and the life of your child is what is important. After all, if you or your partner held strong religious beliefs that fall under my husband's perception about opinions, you probably would not have married.

Notes:_____

_____

_____

_____

_____

_____

_____

_____

_____

22 - Your Child Is Still Defiant!

When nothing seems to help, I go and look at a stonecutter hammering away at his rock perhaps a hundred times without as much as a crack showing in it. Yet at the hundred and first blow it will split in two, and I know it was not that blow that did it, but all that had gone before.

Jacob Riis

You and your partner have read this book, following all the suggestions, but your child is still not listening, is still angry, is not doing his homework and is just blatantly defiant! What do you do?

Take a step back and assess how you and your partner are intervening with your discipline. Are you engaging in power struggles, are you yelling, threatening, taking away everything, etc.? If the answer is, "yes" to any and all, the first thing to do is STOP! Stop the threats, stop the yelling and entering into the power struggles and stop taking away everything. It is obvious that your child is not responding to your requests and is even showing signs of not caring about the consequences. Remember, if your child is repeating the same inappropriate patterns then the discipline you chose is not working. The goal is to find out why. Are your consequences relating to the "crime"? Are you and your partner consistent and following through with your consequences? Are you and your partner losing control of your emotions when disciplining your child?

I have worked with many children, especially those in foster care, where no matter how appropriate or consistent the consequences were, the children continued to be defiant and disrespectful. I helped these families by learning the source of the defiance. Your child does not want to be defiant but has tremendous emotional issues preventing them from understanding how to react appropriately. If your child is struggling with your household limits and rules, chances are your child is behaving inappropriately at school as well. Your child's school is there to help you. Call your child's school and schedule a time to meet with your child's teachers to gain their support. Your child's teachers may have ideas for correcting the negative behavior and can help implement a consistent approach at home and school.

If your child is behaving appropriately at school, perhaps your child has peer issues or something is causing the negative behavior from the home environment. Has there been a recent change in finances, locations, employment, etc. Are you and your partner fighting more? Are you or your partner taking on more responsibilities at work, causing one of you to not be home as often? There could be one or any number of reasons for you to explore to rule in or rule out. After exploring every possible reason and implementing a new discipline strategy based on your conclusions, the negative behavior may still continue. What now?

Implement Attainable Goals For Your Child

Sometimes when things are stressful and all hope for the desired behavior feels lost, we focus on the negatives and not the positives. If you constantly feel you are disciplining your child, some things you can do are:

- Learn to let things go that are not life threatening or detrimental to someone's safety.
- Focus on the positives and praise often.
- Set obtainable goals for your child.
- Spend time with your child that is fun and enjoyable.
- Reward appropriate behavior with praise and affection or special time together.

Lastly and most importantly during this clearly stressful endeavor to correct your child's behavior, always remember to take care of yourself and your partner. When you are faced with a difficult child it can be quite exhausting and challenging. "In families with children who are difficult to control, mothers are likely to function as crisis managers who must cope on a daily basis with a range of dilemmas and conflicts. Often fathers in such families withdraw to avoid dealing with unpleasant situations." (Owens 188) Make sure you and your partner find some time together where you can regroup and enjoy each other's company. During this time do not talk about your difficult child! Use this time to reconnect as a couple. After your diversion is over return home to resume your lives as parents, hopefully rejuvenated from your brief distraction.

Notes:_____

_____

_____

_____

_____

_____

23 - Final Message Of Encouragement

*Those who are lifting the world upward and onward
are those who encourage more than criticize.*

Elizabeth Harrison

Brad and I want to thank you for taking the time to read our book. Our hope is that through this book, you will have the tools necessary to give your children the happy childhood memories they deserve. Many parents in my private practice have asked me to refer a good parenting book and before "Good Parents Bad Parenting" I never felt any other book adequately addressed most of my client's parenting concerns. Keep this book somewhere handy when your parenting experience becomes difficult. Use it as a reference guide and support to help make the rough patches seem a little less rough. As I say to my clients, "I cannot solve all of your problems, because life happens and there are always going to be issues. What I can do is give you the tools necessary to be better equipped to cope with life's problems." When you apply what you have learned from "Good Parents Bad Parenting", I am confident you will feel it provides you with the foundation and tools necessary to be the best parent, partner and person you can be.

Brad and I leave you with wishes for much success and happiness on your parenting journey!

References

Babb, L. Anne, and Rita Laws. <u>Adopting and Advocating for the Special Needs Child: A Guide for Parents and Professionals</u>. Westport, CT: Bergin & Garvey, 199 .

Marc H. Bornstein, ed. <u>Handbook of Parenting</u>. Vol. . Mahwah, NJ: Lawrence Erlbaum Associates, 1995.

Marc H. Bornstein, ed. <u>Handbook of Parenting</u>. Vol. 4. Mahwah, NJ: Lawrence Erlbaum Associates, 1995.

Bossard, James H. S., and Eleanor Stoker Boll. <u>One Marriage, Two Faiths: Guidance on Interfaith Marriage</u>. New York: Ronald Press Co., 195 .

Bowlby, John. <u>A Secure Base: Parent Child Attachment and Healthy Human Development</u>. New York: Basic Books, 1988.

Bradley, Robert H., et al. "Dimensions of Parenting in Families Having Children with Disabilities." <u>Exceptionality</u> 2.1 (1991): 41 61.

Brazelton, T. Berry. <u>To Listen to a Child: Understanding the Normal Problems of Growing Up</u>. Reading, MA: Perseus Books, 1984.

Campbell, Janis M. "Parenting Classes: Focus on Discipline." <u>Journal of Community Health Nursing</u> 9.4 (1992): 19 208.

Carson, David K., and Mark T. Bittner. "Temperament and School Aged Children's Coping Abilities and Responses to Stress." <u>Journal of Genetic Psychology</u> 155. (1994): 289 02.

Good Parents Bad Parenting

Cherlin, Andrew J., and Frank F. Furstenberg. The New American Grandparent: A Place in the Family, a Life Apart. New York: Basic Books, 1992.

Cotterill, Pamela. "'But for freedom, you see, not to be a babyminder': women's attitudes towards grandmother care." Sociology 26.4 (1992): 60 +.

Cowan, Carolyn Pape, and Philip A. Cowan. When Partners Become Parents: The Big Life Change for Couples. Mahwah, NJ: Lawrence Erlbaum Associates, 1999.

Davis, Kimberly. "Parenting in the fast lane: Harry and Donna Coaxum balance high powered, corporate positions with raising a daughter." Ebony Oct. 2002: 114+.

Debating Children's Lives: Current Controversies On Children And Adolescents, edited by Mary Ann Mason and Eileen Gambrill. Thousand Oaks, CA: Sage Publications, 1994.

Forehand, Rex, Nicholas Long, and Gene Brody. "8 Divorce and Marital Conflict: Relationship to Adolescent Competence and Adjustment in Early Adolescence." Impact of Divorce, Single Parenting, and Stepparenting on Children. Ed. E. Mavis Hetherington. Hillsdale, NJ: Lawrence Erlbaum Associates, 1988. 155 168.

Foston, Nikitta A. "Striking a balance: parenting, working and loving."

    Ebony Apr. 200 : 1 2+.

Friedman, M. M. Family nursing: Theory and assessment. Norwalk, CT:

    Apple CenturyCrofts, (1986).

Gottman, John M., Lynn Fainsilber Katz, and Carole Hooven. Meta

    Emotion: How Families Communicate Emotionally. Mahwah,

    NJ: Lawrence Erlbaum Associates, 199 .

E. Mavis Hetherington, ed. Coping with Divorce, Single Parenting, and

    Remarriage: A Risk and Resiliency Perspective. Mahwah, NJ:

    Lawrence Erlbaum Associates, 1999.

E. Mavis Hetherington, ed. Impact of Divorce, Single Parenting, and

    Stepparenting on Children. Hillsdale, NJ: Lawrence Erlbaum

    Associates, 1988.

Barry S. Hewlett, ed. Father Child Relations: Cultural and Biosocial

    Contexts. New York: Aldine De Gruyter, 1992.

Hill, Lilian H. "My child has a learning disability. Now what." Adult

    Learning 12.2 (2001): 24+.

Justice, Blair, and Rita Justice. The Abusing Family. New York: Perseus

    Publishing, 1990.

Kersey, K. C. Don't take it out on your kids: A parent's and teacher's

    guide to positive discipline. Washington, DC: Acropolis Books.

    1990.

Michael E. Lamb, ed. <u>Parenting and Child Development in "Nontraditional" Families</u>. Mahwah, NJ: Lawrence Erlbaum Associates, 1999.

Larsen, Ann Claire. "Governing families with young children through discipline." <u>Journal of Sociology</u> 5. (1999): 2 9.

Leitenberg, Harold, Mark J. Detzer, and Debra Srebnik. "Gender differences in masturbation and the relation of masturbation experience in preadolescence and/or early adolescence to sexual behavior and sexual adjustment in young adulthood." <u>Archives of Sexual Behavior</u> 22.2 (199): 8 +.

Leung, Kwok, Sing Lau, and Wai Lim Lam. "Parenting Styles and Academic Achievement: A Cross Cultural Study." <u>Merrill Palmer Quarterly</u> 44.2 (1998): 15 .

Levine, James A., and Todd L. Pittinsky. <u>Working Fathers: New Strategies for Balancing Work and Family</u>. Reading, MA: Addison Wesley, 199 .

Leving, Jeffery M., and Kenneth A. Dachman. <u>Fathers' Rights: Hard Hitting & Fair Advice for Every Father Involved in a Custody Dispute</u>. Eds. Carol Kort, and Ronnie Friedland. New York: Basic Books, 1998.

Lupton, Deborah. "`A love/hate relationship': the ideals and experiences of first time mothers." <u>Journal of Sociology</u> 6.1 (2000): 50.

Good Parents Bad Parenting

Tom Luster, and Lynn Okagaki, eds. <u>Parenting: An Ecological Perspective</u>. Hillsdale, NJ: Lawrence Erlbaum Associates, 199 .

Mackey, Richard A., and Bernard A. O'Brien. <u>Lasting Marriages: Men and Women Growing Together</u>. Westport, CT: Praeger, 1995.

McCabe, Allyssa. <u>Language Games to Play with Your Child: Enhancing Communication from Infancy through Late Childhood</u>. New York: Perseus Publishing, 1992.

Mccluskey, Ken, and Andrea Mccluskey. "Gray Matters: The Power of Grandparent Involvement." <u>Reclaiming Children and Youth</u> 9.2 (2000): 111.

McLanahan S., & Sandefur G. <u>Growing up with a single parent: What hurts, what helps?</u> Cambridge, MA: Harvard University Press. (1994).

McLanahan, Sara, and Julien Teitler. "Chapter 5 The Consequences of Father Absence." <u>Parenting and Child Development in "Nontraditional" Families</u>. Ed. Michael E. Lamb. Mahwah, NJ: Lawrence Erlbaum Associates, 1999. 8 100.

"Modern parenting: sharing the load." <u>Ebony</u> Apr. 199 : 4+.

Nussbaum, Jon F., et al. <u>Communication and Aging</u>. 2nd ed. Mahwah, NJ: Lawrence Erlbaum Associates, 2000.

Owens, Karen. Raising Your Child's Inner Self Esteem: The Authoritative
  Guide from Infancy through the Teen Years. New York: Perseus
  Publishing, 1995.

Peters, Joan K. When Mothers Work: Loving Our Children without
  Sacrificing Our Selves. Reading, MA: Addison Wesley, 199 .

Popenoe, David. "A world without fathers." The Wilson Quarterly Spring
  1996: 12+.

Popkin, Michael H. Active Parenting: For Parents of 2 to 12 Year Olds
  Parent's Guide Atlanta, GA: Active Parenting, 199 .

Raveis, Victoria H., Karolynn Siegel, and Daniel Karus. "Children's
  psychological distress following the death of a parent." Journal
  of Youth and Adolescence 28.2 (1999): 165.

Sartor, Carolyn E., and James Youniss. "The relationship between positive
  parental involvement and identity achievement during
  adolescence." Adolescence   .146 (2002): 221+.

Shulman, Shmuel, et al. "Coping styles of learning disabled adolescents
  and their parents." Journal of Youth and Adolescence 24.
  (1995): 281+.

Thomas J. Socha, and Glen H. Stamp, eds. Parents, Children and
  Communication: Frontiers of Theory and Research. Mahwah,
  NJ: Lawrence Erlbaum Associates, 1995.

Straus, Murray A., and Glenda Kaufman Kantor. "Corporal punishment of adolescents by parents: a risk factor in the epidemiology of depression, suicide, alcohol abuse, child abuse, and wife beating." Adolescence 29.115 (1994): 54 +.

Thompson, Martie P., et al. "Role of secondary stressors in the parental death child distress relation." Journal of Abnormal Child Psychology 26.5 (1998): 5 .

Troubling Children: Studies of Children and Social Problems. New York: Aldine De Gruyter, 1994.

Walker, Nicole. "Parenting in the '90s: sharing the joy and the duties." Ebony Aug. 1998: 52+.

Wenz Gross, Melodie, and Gary N. Siperstein. "Students with learning problems at risk in middle school: stress, social support, and adjustment." Exceptional Children 65.1 (1998): 91+.

Wesselmann, Debra. The Whole Parent: How to Become a Terrific Parent Even If You Didn't Have One. New York: Perseus Publishing, 1998.

Wetzstein, Cheryl. "All together under one roof: Fathers bill aims to keep 'fragile' families from splitting up." The Washington Times 1 Nov. 1999: .

Winfield, Fairlee E. Commuter Marriage: Living Together, Apart. New York: Columbia University Press, 1985.

Printed in the United States
101650LV00004B/101/A